Praise for *Hunting Discomfort*

"A step-by-step guide to empower and equip us with the ability to handle anything and everything."

—SHANNON KAISER, International Mindset Coach and bestselling author of *Return to You*

"Data can give you a direction, but the actions in *Hunting Discomfort* will take you there."

—SCOTT TAYLOR, The Data Whisperer, MetaMeta Consulting

"The best part of life is learning to live in your discomfort. Sterling Hawkins's book gives you the tools to achieve your ultimate potential."

—MARGIE HABER, celebrity acting coach, mentor and author of *F*ck Your Comfort Zone*

"More than a book, *Hunting Discomfort* is an emotionally engaging and practical leadership tool written by a man who lives its wisdom. It will take you on an intimate journey of self-discovery and reveal blind spots holding you back from growth. Embrace its teachings and prepare for breakthroughs you've never thought possible."

—LT. COL. WALDO WALDMAN, decorated fighter pilot and author of the *New York Times* **and** *Wall Street Journal* **bestseller** *Never Fly Solo*

"To win, we need to play offense and hunt discomfort instead of waiting until it seeks us out, underprepared, under-skilled and even unready in today's all-too-uncertain world. Hawkins not only proves it, but shows you the way."

—PAUL EPSTEIN, bestselling author of *The Power of Playing Offense*, **leadership keynote speaker, former NFL and NBA executive**

"Discomfort, like it or not, is where all growth happens. Instead of waiting until you or your company 'need' to grow, this book gives you the keys to unlock that growth on your terms, so you're able to call on it no matter what stands in your way."

—RYAN ESTIS, Ryan Estis & Associates

"Facing our fears and turning over the stones that we usually avoid is made so much easier with Sterling's philosophy! If you've ever longed for a watertight process to help you reach your absolute potential, *Hunting Discomfort* is it!"
—**SEBASTIAN TERRY, founder, 100things**

"We all have goals we want to achieve. And in between where we are now and where we long to be, there's a long list of reasons, excuses and justifications. We must get past those obstacles to live the life we want. This book shows you the way."
—**TED RYCE, celebrity trainer and host of the *Legendary Life* podcast**

"While many books promise to inspire and motivate, this one actually gives you the tools to do the things you dream of doing. Hawkins masterfully weaves personal stories together with science-backed research and real-world examples to give any reader the reigns to drive results."
—**JOHN LIVESAY, sales keynote speaker, author of *The Sale is in the Tale* and host of *The Successful Pitch* podcast**

"Change in the world today is not only constant, but speeding up! It's unavoidable and often difficult and unexpected. During these times, Hawkins shares the keys to keep up and break through with practices that anyone can grab onto and use to immediately inject transformative results. The steps he shares will unleash the ultimate potential inside any reader and any organization."
—**CASSANDRA WORTHY, speaker, author and CEO of Change Enthusiasm Global**

"It's easy to opt for more comfort and certainty in health, life and business. This book breaks the mold and shows how we not only need discomfort, but can use it as a pathway to the results that we've always dreamed of. A critical read for midlife males and anyone with a drive to reach that next level."
—**GREG SCHEINMAN, speaker, performance coach and author of *The Midlife Male***

"No company (or person) can afford to stay purely in their comfort zone; the world today demands more, faster and better from all of us. *Hunting Discomfort* flips the paradigm on discomfort with tools and exercises to build a growth mindset in individuals, teams and company cultures to create breakthrough results no matter what the world throws at them."
—**CHRIS DIERINGER, general manager, Retail & Consumer Goods, Microsoft**

"Innovation is about having the creative courage to dare to dream what others cannot—not an easy task in the face of tech disruption, civil unrest and even global uncertainty. Hawkins captures the essence of what it really takes to innovate, to change and grow at a time when many individuals, companies and the world need it more than ever."

—**SARA FRASCA, award-winning entrepreneur, former corporate executive and owner of business coaching firm Point Northeast**

"*Hunting Discomfort* isn't a work of feel-good platitudes but a lifetime accumulation of transformative advice to help each of us find the breakthroughs we're looking for. I couldn't recommend this book and the work of Sterling more highly. If you are sick and tired of the stagnation that accompanies the status quo in life, this book will put an end to it and bring you to greater heights of fulfillment."

—**JOHNNY KING, men's coach, bestselling author and podcast host of *Becoming Kings***

"The twenty-first century is being reshaped at an accelerated and unprecedented pace, but Sterling Hawkins reminds us that our ability to achieve our own human potential has not changed. With the tools he lays out in *Hunting Discomfort*, we have a greater opportunity to embrace challenges and create meaningful and impactful experiences in the workplace."

—**ERIC RODRIGUEZ, chief of staff, Intel**

"My mind is blown to see how Sterling has brilliantly captured a framework to enable anyone to hunt discomfort confidently and with excitement for what might be on the other side."

—**TOM FURPHY, CEO, Consumer Equity Partners**

"This is a book about the truth. The truths that make us, chase us, find us and eventually can transform us. Sterling writes from a place of experience and life lived—he uses his own scars to point us toward the discomfort we didn't know we needed but will forever be changed by. Read it. Share it. Embrace it. You'll be glad you did."

—**CHRIS FIELD, founder of Mercy Project and business professor, Texas A&M University**

HUNTING
DISCOMFORT

STERLING HAWKINS

WONDERWELL

Library of Congress Control Number: 2021919686

ISBN 978-1-63756-014-3 (hardcover)
ISBN 978-1-63756-015-0 (EPUB)

Editor: Joanna Henry
Cover design: Ashish Joshi
Interior design: Morgan Krehbiel
Author photo: Gabe Montero

Published by Wonderwell in Los Angeles, CA
www.wonderwell.press

WONDERWELL

Distributed in the US by Publishers Group West and in Canada by Publishers Group Canada

Printed and bound in Canada

To my grandmother, who demonstrated each and every day she was alive that we're all capable of accomplishing extraordinary things—through hardships, trials or struggles—no matter what.

And to all those who are courageous enough to step out of their head and into their heart.

Contents

CHAPTER 1

Hunting Discomfort

The way out is through.

—My mom. Also, Robert Frost.

"PLEASE WELCOME TO THE STAGE—Sterling Hawkins."

The master of ceremonies had just stepped to the podium to make the announcement. The Singapore conference center was at maximum capacity as he addressed the hundreds of participants of the Seamless Asia conference. I don't remember much of what he said before I heard my name. I was consumed by the tension that was rippling through my body, leaving a pit in my stomach and my fingers trembling. I'd been afraid before, but this felt like something that went far beyond any definition of fear that I knew. All I had going for me was that I was wearing a suit, so the sweat now soaking my shirt wasn't visible. If my name and face weren't plastered all over the place announcing me as the keynote speaker, I would have bolted in those moments before being called onto that stage and into my worst nightmare.

To say I wasn't a professional speaker would have been an understatement. I have always been one of those people who would rather be in the coffin than giving the eulogy. Even though I had worked my tail off preparing and practicing for this moment, that didn't seem to help my nerves. Clearly, I had made a terrible mistake and needed to get out of there! But before I could flee the scene, I heard the introduction I'd been anxiously anticipating for months.

It was too late . . . and good thing. It ended up being the breakthrough moment that led me from a being part of a multibillion-dollar bankruptcy—which had left me anxiety-ridden, single, depressed and playing out a sad country song of living at my parents' house while in my thirties—to an entirely new path of hunting down and working through discomfort to realize breakthroughs beyond my wildest dreams.

Since that moment, I've become a professional keynote speaker presenting on stages around the world. I've given a TEDx Talk sharing how we can all go through discomfort in order to reach our goals, dreams and ambitions. And I've used those practices to aid in the launch, growth and investment of more than fifty companies and with hundreds of people from the #NoMatterWhat Community (more on that later). It turns out there's something of a formula for engineering breakthroughs. The key ingredient? Discomfort.

Over the past decade, I've been developing this formula through my own series of personal experiments with proactively seeking discomfort. I've sought physical discomfort like running fifty miles and cycling through the Rocky Mountains, emotional and mental discomfort such as having tough conversations and sharing failures publicly, and even spiritual discomfort through plant medicine ceremonies deep in the jungles of Peru (most of *that* experience would make for a different book entirely).

As unbelievable as my life has become, this book isn't about me. It's about you. And it's the amalgamation of thousands of hours of training, coaching and mentoring poured into me by some of the most incredible people I've ever met. That, and of the pursuit of learning everything I could through the available research and studies in order to fine-tune a process for hunting discomfort for breakthrough results. I've done it. Others have done it. You can do it, too.

Before we head off for the hunt, let's take a moment to discuss why discomfort is so important, especially in our increasingly uncertain world.

Discomfort—Our Feedback System

So many of us fantasize about having perfect lives in a perfect world. Many of us believe that once we reach a certain point in our business, career or relationship—or number in our bank account—we will finally be free of struggle, constraints and pain. I hate to be the bearer of tough news here, but you're fantasizing about a fantasy. As doctor Gabor Maté, author of *In the Realm of Hungry Ghosts* writes, "You're looking for security and think that will give you freedom."[1] Discomfort is fundamentally necessary, and denying it or attempting to avoid it leaves you at a severe disadvantage.

You've probably heard of leprosy. Left turn here, I know. It'll make sense in a minute. The bacteria that cause leprosy, officially known as Hansen's disease, was first discovered in 1873 by Norwegian physician G.A. Hansen. It's an awful disease that, untreated, will leave the afflicted with muscle weakness, skin lesions and eventually the loss of nose, toes, fingers and/or limbs. Hansen was surprised to discover that the bacteria wasn't responsible for the loss of extremities. The bacteria damaged nerves, which in turn led to patients losing their sense of physical pain. Without this feedback system to monitor an injury, the patients often wouldn't know how serious the injury was. Their wounds would become further damaged and infected, eventually resulting in tissue death.

Physical pain is one form of discomfort, but all discomfort, whether physical, mental, emotional or even spiritual, works in a similar way—it is our feedback system. Without discomfort we are unable to detect how we're interacting with the environment, assess current or pending danger, or handle things that need attention.

Discomfort—Our Compass

Discomfort helps us stay oriented in the world. Like the needle of a compass, it points the way of our path forward.

Today we live in a world of accelerating disruption, incredible complexity and increasing risks, unknowns on a global scale. You feel it around you, don't you? The COVID-19 pandemic, tech disruption, civil unrest, misinformation, environmental challenges, corporate restructurings, changing working conditions, and at the same time increasing demands from customers, communities and, I'm willing to bet, family.

We are increasingly forced to grapple with the unknown in all areas of our lives. The maps we've used in the past to successfully navigate the world often do not reflect the rapidly changing landscape, leaving us with obsolete navigational systems.

At the edge of everything you know personally and we know collectively is the unknown. When you cross over that edge, you may encounter a feeling of chaos that most people are trying to avoid: discomfort. You might recognize it with some of the same feelings I had before being called to the stage in Singapore. A pit in your stomach, trembling limbs, words of fear, anxiety, anger or worry not entirely capturing the moment.

As uncomfortable as it is, we don't get a pass from facing the unknown and its harbinger, change. It's an inherent part of life. Most people hear that as bad news. The truth is, on the other side of the unknown are all the results you are looking for. What news could be better than that? When you turn toward discomfort, you will discover a compass leading you to what you want most.

Avoiding Discomfort Means You'll Have to Live with It

Whenever I introduce the concept of hunting discomfort in workshops, there is always someone who initially bristles at it and insists they don't have to hunt discomfort, they're already surrounded by it!

Yes, true. Whether it's difficult relationships, business challenges, health issues or something else—we all have discomfort in our lives without having to go out looking for it. And usually so much discomfort that priority number one is just getting some relief, not looking for more.

Here's the harsh reality: you're not dealing with your discomfort. If you have that much discomfort coming at you, that means that on some level (or every level) you're trying to avoid it rather than doing something about it. And, by the way, the doing something about it is the hunting discomfort part. Because if you don't deal with your current discomforts, you're accepting a lifetime sentence of living with them.

You ever hear the saying "Better the devil you know?" Well, here is that devil. Most of us prefer to stick with the particular (and familiar) discomfort we already have than face the discomfort of something new. After all, anything new is unknown! In practice, this looks like delaying tough conversations, putting up with jobs we don't like or struggling financially to make ends meet.

And you guessed it, avoiding or delaying discomfort leaves you with the same results you've always had. And likely the same complaints about them: "I don't have enough money," "There aren't enough hours in the day!" "If I just had [*fill in the blank*], everything would be okay."

That's not hunting discomfort; that's living with it.

Discomfort doesn't sound so unappetizing now, does it?

Unleashing the Power of the Unknown

If you want to accomplish any breakthrough for yourself, things are going to get uncomfortable at times. It is going to require figuring out how to do things that you haven't done before. Hopefully no surprise there. But this is where tapping into the unknown works to your advantage—starting with the unknown power that resides within you.

When researchers first started studying the brain, they expected to see vast amounts of information-processing power. They found it, but not where you might expect. Although our subconscious mind— below consciousness or awareness—is able to process millions of bits of information from our eyes, ears, skin and other senses, most of it is lost to what we're actually aware of.[2] In fact, our conscious mind filters out all but about 0.00000455 percent of it. That's like having a super-computer but instead using an abacus!

Although we might not consciously be aware of it, that super-computer has answers for you. The challenge is that it speaks in sensations, images and emotions—some of which might be downright unpleasant (remember all those symptoms of discomfort?).

If you ignore these subconscious messages, perceived threats from the past will be continually reintroduced until you're ready to process and resolve them. I'm not a doctor, but it seems to me that those ghosts of the past might be linked with the anxiety epidemic that appears to be sweeping the planet.

When you do tap into the vast resource of the subconscious, you open yourself up to opportunities for discovering ideas, connections and resolutions that may be entirely new—to you, or to the world.

From Embracing Discomfort to Hunting It

Here's where it gets interesting. We are not limited to working only with the discomfort that arises naturally. After all, most people have designed their lives to avoid discomfort, so much so that they might not even know where it is anymore. So we're going to have to proactively hunt it to find the greatest rewards. Discomfort is a divining rod that can point you directly where you need to go in order to find what you're searching for, be it more money, a growing business, closer relationships or even more joy.

Waiting for discomfort to find you is like waiting to work out until you happen to be in a gym. You limit your opportunities to work out and grow stronger in all the other moments of your life. Hunting discomfort works the same way. The more situations in which you practice engaging with discomfort, the better you get at dealing with it in any situation. It's a muscle you can build.

Discomfort is discomfort: whether physical, mental or emotional, our biological and neurological responses to any form of discomfort are nearly identical.

Researchers at the University of Michigan published an article in *Science* titled "Does Rejection Hurt?" Using the latest brain scanning technology, they found that the brain signatures of processing emotional discomfort were nearly identical to those resulting from processing physical injury.[3]

Further, the treatment for different types of discomfort appears to be interchangeable. Physicians published a study in *Psychological Science* showing that taking acetaminophen reduces emotional pain as well as physical pain because the brain uses the same neural (or very similar) pathways to process discomfort.[4]

Now, I'm not suggesting that you pop a Tylenol the next time your feelings are hurt, but I am asserting that if our cognitive processes are similar for different types of discomforts, then we may be able to identify some universal responses for embracing any type of discomfort.

Hunting discomfort strengthens what I call your "discomfort muscle," increasing your capacity to handle greater and greater levels of discomfort. By hunting that discomfort, you expose yourself to the unknown and naturally build the courage required to deal with it. Or, stating it from a more scientific standpoint, increase the ability of your nervous system to get comfortable with the uncomfortable.

This brings me back to Singapore . . .

The Way Out Is Through

Being in Singapore to speak at that conference wasn't a mistake. I had deliberately sought out the experience without really understanding why. (This was the genesis of my hunting discomfort path, don't forget.) All I knew was that I was at a moment in my life where I had hit rock bottom and I had to do something, anything, to break the complacency of despair that had taken ahold of me.

I'd just been on one hell of a roller-coaster ride. I'd started a company right out of college with my dad. We sold it to a group in Silicon Valley and it went on to become part of the Apple Pay before Apple Pay (a biometric payment service where you scan your finger for access to an electronic wallet). We raised 550 million dollars at a multibillion-dollar valuation, had offices all over the world and employed over seven hundred people. I was riding high with first-class plane tickets, a swanky office, a gorgeous girlfriend and a penthouse apartment just waiting for me. It was like a scene from *The Wolf of Wall Street*! And then the global housing market collapsed, our investments dried up and, within a blink of an eye, I was jobless and broke, and my girlfriend had broken up with me. Hopped up on anxiety medication, I went from penthouse to parents' house. I was so attached to what I thought I knew about myself and the world that I was left questioning if I could go on or if I even wanted to.

That's where I was the day I was listlessly staring at the computer screen and a spam message about a business conference randomly popped up. At that moment, one of my mom's sayings immediately came to mind. She used a lot of adages when I was a kid, like "It's cheaper to milk a cow than buy one." What? Or "Don't take any wooden nickels." I still don't know what that means. But the saying that came to mind that day—and suddenly made perfect sense—was "The way out is through." (Okay, it turns out that's actually a quote from Robert Frost, but to me it will always be my mom's.)

If I wanted to get out of the situation I was in, I had to go through discomfort. Without thinking, I clicked on the reply button of the spam message and wrote, "Why don't you have me speak? Best, Sterling." Before too long, I got a message back from the conference organizer, offering to discuss my suggestion, and after several conversations, I was offered the opportunity to be the conference's keynote speaker! I accepted—terrified—and then worked my tail off on the presentation and tried to acclimate to the severe discomfort I had of public speaking. All through those months leading up to the conference I was driven by the unrelenting discomfort and fear of what I had agreed to take on.

Only when I stepped off the stage after delivering my address did I finally feel some blessed relief. I think I had blacked out during part of the speech, I was so nervous. What a journey it had been! Little did I know the journey was actually just starting. The conference director sought me out immediately, despite my attempt to hide from him. He looked me in the eye and said, "Sterling, that's the best talk I've seen in all my years of doing this!" To this day I'm not entirely convinced he heard the same talk I gave, but I will remain ever grateful to him for the chance to speak at the conference and for going on to refer me through his networks. With some hard work and more discomfort than I knew existed, I pushed through and on the other side I discovered a brand-new career.

As I started to realize that the way out is through discomfort, I began to look for it anywhere and everywhere. I found it in stories throughout history (many of which you'll read in this book), and in all corners of the globe, including as I trekked the Sahara, went cage-diving with great white sharks near Seal Island, close to Cape Town, and experienced many other adventures with my with #NoMatterWhat Community members. With each step on the journey, I felt myself and those around me getting stronger.

Discomfort vs. Danger

Where do you draw the line with discomfort? To be clear, discomfort is not the same thing as danger. It's simply discomfort. Feeling the feelings of discomfort—in whatever form they come in—and doing whatever is causing the discomfort anyway is the core of growth.

Danger on the other hand, is when there is a very real possibility of causing injury or harm to yourself or others. Above I wrote that I went cage-diving with the great whites. Notice the word *cage*. I didn't recklessly throw myself in with the sharks. Hunting discomfort and putting yourself in the way of danger are very different things, in action and in spirit. It's mindful versus mindless. People seeking danger often do it for the rush. Whereas we hunt discomfort for the growth.

Real Danger vs. Perceived Danger

Truth be told, most of us are not in any real trouble of seeking too much danger. Rather, we can experience a high degree of discomfort that is out of proportion to the actual danger involved. Let's take skydiving, for example. Before I ever jumped from a plane, it seemed like a very dangerous form of entertainment. When one year my sister insisted that we go skydiving for her birthday, I thought she was insane. What kind of people do that? I agreed, though reluctantly.

My fear about leaping out of planes had nothing to do with the actual dangers of skydiving. In 2020, the United States Parachute Association reported that 0.0004 percent of jumps in the country resulted in fatality. In 2019, the average person in the United States had a better chance of dying from a bee sting (0.0017 percent chance), a lightning strike (0.007 percent) or a car accident (0.93 percent).[5] Whatever activity has you petrified probably has little to do with the actual danger involved. What we know about something and how doing it (or the thought of doing it) feels aren't always aligned.

The more you hunt discomfort, the better you will become at facing your fears and being able to easily distinguish between real and perceived dangers, which means you will know when to take a risk and when playing it safe is the smart move.

Before We Jump In . . .

Lately, I've been taking swimming lessons to be a stronger competitive freestyle swimmer. There are libraries with shelves full of books about swimming. I could study the topic for years: the physics of it, perfect motion, best practices—I could go so far as get a PhD in it. But all that knowledge wouldn't matter much the first time I get thrown into a pool.

We live in a time when just about all human knowledge is accessible from one's mobile phone. The "secrets" to nearly anything you want to accomplish have been written many times over. The results are not in knowledge alone. It's about shedding the discomfort that is standing in the way of your applying that tremendous knowledge you have (or could easily acquire).

You know this. Any meaningful new result you've created didn't come from just from thinking about it. You had to summon the courage to risk confronting the unknown head-on. Maybe it took making that risky presentation, declaring that audacious goal and working toward it, or even embarrassing yourself as you tried to do something new you hoped would eventually lead to some level of success. Whatever it was, you had to go through that discomfort in order to come out the other side.

Discomfort is the only thing that's between you and the results that you want. Period. Otherwise, you would have it already. You've spent enough time coping with discomforts, medicating them or avoiding them completely. And justifying why you still don't have the results that you want. I know I have. If you're looking for a book that's going to explain away any of those less-than-pleasant feelings, this book's not for you. Not only are we not going to explain them away or find ways to not deal with them, we're going to go one step further. It's time to take discomfort head-on and go through it.

In this book, I'm going to walk you through the step-by-step practice I've developed for hunting discomfort. On the journey, we'll examine five key discomforts that keep us stuck:

1. The discomfort of reality and how our feelings are primed to distort it.
2. The discomfort of self-doubt and its paralyzing grip on our results.
3. The discomfort of exposure and going after what you really want.
4. The discomfort of challenges, obstacles and roadblocks.
5. And, ultimately, the discomfort that rules all the discomforts listed above: uncertainty around what's coming next.

For each one, I will provide you with the practice designed to hunt that specific discomfort, so you can achieve whatever goal you might have—no matter what is standing in your way. But you have to really want that goal. It's not for everyone, and it's not for all the time. It's for when you're stagnated, overwhelmed or confused about what your next step should be. Or maybe you're just tired of the same old results. Either way, you have to be all-in for this practice to work.

If you're ready to get started, here's your first challenge. Grab a pen right now and answer the following question.

Imagine the contents of this book will change your life. What would that look like? (Go ahead and dream big for your company, community or family. No reason to hold back.)

Here's the thing: this book can absolutely help you, however audacious your dreams—*if* (and only if) you use it correctly. For its maximum effectiveness, I suggest you:

- Find a place you can focus on reading with few distractions.
- Read at least ten minutes a day until you're finished with the book.
- Have a notebook and pen handy. Work on the exercises as soon as you encounter them in the text. Don't just keep reading, thinking you'll come back to them. You probably won't. Face the discomfort head-on.
- Commit to reading this entire book and having it be a turning point in your life.

To that last point, do it right now. Commitment is a key component of success.

Are you ready to commit? Fill in the following.

I, _____*(your name), commit to working through this book and embracing the discomfort along the way in service to my goals, dreams and aspirations.*

Signature: _____

Date: _____

Warning: This book will (by necessity) be disruptive to you, your identity and your beliefs. If you're going to get what you want, you have to change. The threat to your identity might predispose you to write off or disagree with some of the material. You might become fixated on some anomaly as a way of unwittingly protecting your current views. That protective element might be exactly what has been in your way. To get the most out of this book, try these ideas on like you would a new shirt. See how they fit and see how they feel. Even if they conflict with something else you've heard.

But before we head out . . . did you skip over the section where you agree to make this book work best for you? Did you ignore it or only half-heartedly agree? If so, you have a chance to practice hunting discomfort right now. You do it by going back and making that commitment to yourself. Go on, I'll wait. It makes all the difference.

Time to Jump

Don't worry, it's not all doom and discomfort. Along the journey you'll start to realize something that I first learned during a shark dive outside Cape Town.

I'd been sitting in a small boat under the hot African sun for hours and hours, with not a great white in sight. I resigned myself to the idea that no sharks were coming that day. I put my feet in the water and dug around for a sandwich to snack on while I stared, discouraged and bored, at the horizon.

What happened next is a blur. A sixteen-foot shark leaped eight feet out of the water, its rows of razor-sharp teeth destroying the bait hanging inches from where I was sitting. Again I felt a very visceral fear that words alone don't do justice to. I could hear people screaming. Well, no kidding, the shark *was* terrifying. Except they weren't screaming, they were yelling: "Get in the water now! Get in the water now!" This was exactly the opposite of what I wanted to do. I wanted what we all want when confronted with discomfort—to retreat to safety. In this case, the interior of the boat or, better yet, dry land.

But I took a deep breath, just like you should when you're confronted with discomfort during the coming chapters, and I jumped. In that moment I realized that results aren't the only thing on the other side of discomfort—all the best experiences in life are there as well.

So, take a deep breath.

Now . . . let's jump in, together.

CHAPTER 2

Discomfort #1: Facing Reality

*It's not what you look at that matters,
it's what you see.*

—Henry David Thoreau

THROUGHOUT THE COURSE OF OUR LIVES, we are bombarded by unwelcome realities. Be it a job loss, breakup, business failure, health crisis or pandemic—reality throws some very uncomfortable punches from time to time. Learning how to navigate in a world that is often unpredictable is integral to success.

Just because tomorrow is inherently unknowable, we don't have to resign ourselves to a life of being blindsided or being lost when predictions fail. We are hunters now, and hunters don't wander around lost and waiting to be pounced on—at least not any that I've ever heard of. Besides, not all of reality is outside of our control. How we perceive our reality lies entirely within our domain and has tremendous impact on all our results. That's why the first discomfort we will be exploring is "reality"—and how you see it.

Relative Reality: Our Faulty and Limiting Beliefs

Remember the dress that blew up the Internet? In 2015, a washed-out photo of a dress went viral when viewers couldn't agree on whether the gown was blue with black lace or white with gold lace. Over 11 million tweets were exchanged as people around the globe vehemently argued about what they saw with their own eyes.[1]

No matter what side of the dress debate you were on, the dress *was* a specific color. In reality, it was blue and black—a verifiable fact, confirmed by the manufacturer. The truth about the dress was the truth about the dress.

If only it were always so easy to determine what is true in our reality. Because here's another fact: reality is a thing, even though we may not always see it accurately. That's why things that can be measured, observed and tested are easier to agree upon. Sadly, most of reality is more nuanced and complex than a dress color. Despite this, we spend most of our lives assuming our singular perspective on reality is obvious and immutable.

But what if the incredible market opportunity you've discovered, person you've hired or reason your business is struggling is actually the blue and black dress? In other words, you're out of touch with reality. How would you even know? With the dress it's easy—you can look up the color. Most situations we encounter are far more convoluted. What we're missing is an Internet meme showing us perceptions different from ours and highlighting where we might have a faulty view.

Things that haven't been proven or discovered yet are even *more* difficult to determine with any certainty. As Tufts University psychology professor Raymond Nickerson notes in his paper on confirmation bias, psychological literature seems to support that, when trying to imagine something that doesn't exist or hasn't been done, we fall back on our "preexisting beliefs, expectations, or a hypothesis in hand" to guide our thinking.[2] Makes perfect sense to do so, but it means we are drawing only from the realm of what we already know is possible. In other words, from our limiting beliefs.

Since all results in our lives flow from our actions, and our actions are driven by how we see ourselves and the world, we must identify our faulty and limiting beliefs if we hope to expand. Let's take a closer look at how beliefs and perspectives work.

The Run That Changed Reality

It was the early 1950s and the record for the all-time fastest mile run stood at 4.1 minutes. This record had been unbroken for nearly a decade, and according to the world of sport medicine at the time, that's the way it was going to stay. Humans, it was believed, had reached their physical and biological limitation of speed.

Roger Bannister was a gifted runner from England. He had great success on his Oxford University team, but when his opportunity came to compete in the 1952 Olympics, he didn't even medal. He was devastated and considered giving up running forever. Instead, he decided to expand his understanding of what he could achieve in his sport. He decided to try to run a mile in under four minutes. Despite the popular belief that it simply wasn't possible, Bannister believed it was.

Several months later, Bannister took his position at the starting line of his record-attempt race, along with five others. It was a cold, wet, windy day—the antithesis of good conditions—but it was time to put his new belief into action. The lead was traded several times, but in the last lap Bannister pulled ahead and won the race, collapsing with exhaustion at the finish line. The race announcer began to call out the time: "Three minutes and . . ." The crowd roared to life. They had just witnessed the impossible becoming the possible. Roger had run a mile in 3 minutes and 59.4 seconds.

Roger Bannister forever transformed beliefs about humankind's running potential. It took lifetimes for anyone to break the four-minute mile, yet Bannister's title lasted only forty-six days before someone else beat his time. And then *that* time was beaten. And beaten again. Once Bannister demonstrated that it was possible, others believed it for themselves as well. He freed them from their limiting beliefs—arguably a greater legacy than his record that lasted only forty-six days.

The Lenses of Belief

Dr. Carol Dweck, author of *Mindset*, writes that "in a growth mindset, people believe that their most basic abilities can be developed through dedication and hard work."[3] What's more, what can and cannot be done in the world is driven by what those beliefs are, and often not any objective reality.

There is real power in that statement if you let it sink in, along with real discomfort. Many of us love the idea that we could possess the power to change the world, but when it comes to *responsibility* for the results we're not happy with—not so much. And the assertion that our beliefs, even our most cherished and nonnegotiable ones (actually, *especially* these beliefs), may be up for debate? Hard pass.

Here's where the rubber meets to road: most of the actions you're taking in life are not based on reality, but rather your view of reality. What we all see on the surface is a superficial representation of reality filtered through the lenses of our beliefs, an idea that was developed by the English philosopher and physician John Locke in his book *An Essay Concerning Human Understanding*, published all the way back in 1689.[4]

We tend to be very attached to our beliefs because they look real to us and they inform our identity, making it very difficult to see them for what they are: just a lens—but an important lens. One that is determining all your results in life.

Here is how it works:

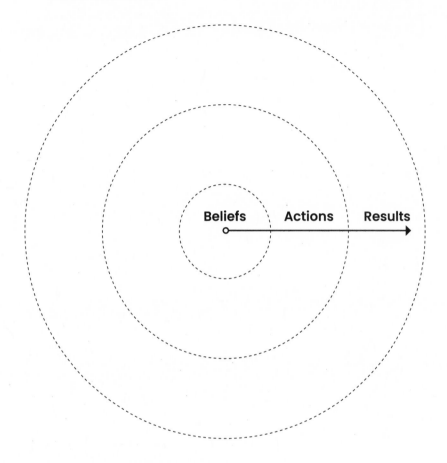

Figure 2.1: The Lens of Belief Driving Action

Beliefs (about yourself, another or the world around you) drive your actions. Actions drive your results.

It really is that simple.

You Can't Change Reality, but You Can Change How You See It

When I was about fifteen, I realized I couldn't see the chalkboard at school anymore. (Yes, it was a chalkboard back in those days.) The news that I needed glasses wasn't exactly welcome. I told myself a lot of stories about what I would be losing once I got glasses: my ability to play soccer, my street cred, and most especially my "cool" looks. (The glasses lenses were as thick as the bottom of Coke bottles!)

But accepting those drawbacks and putting on those new lenses opened up my world to see reality more clearly. I got better results in school, yes, but the impact went far beyond the blackboard. Suddenly, there were the leaves on the trees and stars in the night sky—things that had always been there but that I'd been unable to see clearly. It was like my entire reality got bigger, brighter and more beautiful. And that is what new lenses can do: they radically expand one's view of the world and of what is possible.

After years of wearing corrective glasses and contacts, I've noticed that I take my clear vision for granted. I've gotten used to what I am seeing, and besides, I'm looking through my lenses, not at them. Again, beliefs work in much the same way. We're not usually looking at the belief, we're looking through the belief, so we forget that we are seeing only a version of reality.

Real Change Comes from Changing Your Beliefs

The natural place to look to change something is out in the world. The result you want to get to. For example, if I want more money, I need to work harder. That leads to a business or personal trajectory that typically results in only incremental amounts of change. (See figure 2.2 on page 22.)

If you are hunting real change, then you are going to have to also look inward and start to grapple with some areas of discomfort around your perceptions of yourself, those around you and the world. This type of work can leave you thoroughly disoriented. When you call into question the foundational concepts—from your parents, teachers, bosses, society and even your own experience—that you've invested in and held true, maybe even for most of your life, it may trigger a visceral feeling of being powerless and vulnerable to your core. It's uncomfortable to surrender those views. And to, more powerfully, step across the line to admitting that maybe some of those views are inaccurate or ineffective. And if that's true of one area, you have to confront the uncomfortable fact that you might not be seeing reality in another area, or another, or any of them. Everything can suddenly feel like it is up for grabs—what you're capable of, what's actually possible or impossible and how the world around you works.

If you've ever worn virtual-reality goggles and lost your balance even though your feet were still firmly planted on a solid floor, you'll know what I mean. That's what it can feel like to challenge "your truth"—it can be totally disorienting and confusing. In other words, it will get worse before it gets better. Many people want to be the celebrated phoenix rising from the ashes—but few want to burn. Burn the identity, beliefs, mindsets that created your current results. You have to confront the discomfort of what you don't know and be willing to take on what you learn.

The flip side of all this is that you are opening yourself to a world of pure possibility, cracking open almost limitless potential for yourself and the world around you. It's like free falling into discovery. That's where real and authentic change comes from: your new view.

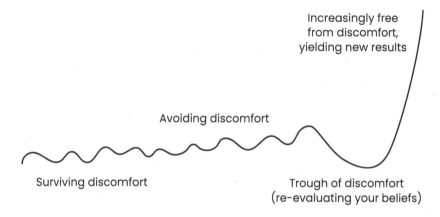

Figure 2.2: Real Change Driven by New Beliefs. Avoiding discomfort leaves you with incremental results. Dramatic change comes from going through the discomfort of changing your beliefs.

The Origin and Nature of Lenses of Belief

Lenses of belief all come from the same place: the past. Your upbringing, your parents, what you've lived through, your culture have all contributed to forming your current structure of beliefs and perspectives. In fact, most of our core beliefs are established by the time we're seven years old![5] Using the past is useful to understand what works and what doesn't work. The problem is the past is not always a great predictor of what might work in the future. This is why many of our unexamined beliefs can actually be holding us back.

If you're from central New York State, like I am, you probably know what a pike is—a famously aggressive, carnivorous fish. When placed in a tank with smaller fish, the pike will immediately devour them.

German zoologist Karl Möbius was a pioneer in the field of ecology who conducted a groundbreaking experiment back in the 1800s, when he was a director at the Museum für Naturkunde in Berlin.[6] It's been replicated many times since, and it's an experiment I first read about in Josh Linkner's *New York Times* bestselling book *Disciplined Dreaming*.

Researchers placed a glass barrier in the tank, separating the pike from the smaller fish. The pike repeatedly smashed itself against the glass but was unable to break through and catch its prey. After a while, the pike stopped bashing its poor nose against the invisible barrier and sank to the bottom of the tank, defeated.

This is where it gets interesting.

The scientists then removed the glass, allowing the pike access to its food once more. To everyone's surprise, it didn't stir. Even when dinner swam directly in front of its mouth, the pike remained listless at the bottom of the tank. It had so thoroughly internalized the invisible barrier and the view that hunting was futile that it—brace yourself—ended up dying of starvation.

This experiment demonstrates the power of faulty lenses and the way past experiences can paralyze, constrain and limit future results. There's now even a name for this kind of thinking: pike syndrome.

Don't Be Pike-Minded

Pike syndrome illustrates a form of faulty lenses or limiting beliefs that may be impacting your results. Although you may or may not be famously aggressive in the circles you run in, you can think of the smaller fish as your goals, your dreams or simply the things you want to achieve. Limiting beliefs based on past experience may be showing up for you in one of three primary ways.

1. I Couldn't Then, So I Can't Now

Just as the pike assumed that since there was previously a glass barrier, there would always be a glass barrier, we too can fall prey to the belief that because we couldn't do something in the past, we also cannot do it now.

Previous business failures may generate a belief that you cannot be successful in future business opportunities.

A tumultuous relationship in the past can lead you to conclude that that's just the way it will always be.

Experiencing the same results for a decade might lead you to believe that the next ten years will be just the same.

Remember, the past has little bearing on the future—unless you allow your past beliefs to create your future.

2. It's Not Worth the Risk

If we personify the pike for a minute, how do you think it felt after all that failure? It might have felt dejected, lost, even embarrassed. Its entire reputation as the baddest of the bad was decimated. Not to mention the physical pain it endured from repeatedly smashing into the wall. Many of us have been there in one way or another, and these experiences can lead to the creation of a lens of belief that makes us more averse to the risk of failure.

Avital S. Cherniawsky, a researcher at the University of Montreal, and Clay B. Holroyd from the University of Victoria, found that the brain automatically overvalues immediate rewards and undervalues future rewards, even if that future reward is much greater.[7] This means that if we are looking through a risk-averse lens, we are going to value our immediate reputation and comfort over the potential success on the other side of risk. We lose our ability to properly assess risk—a skill required by every successful leader—and stay entrenched in our existing conditions, where we believe we are safer and more comfortable. (Until we starve to death, that is.)

3. That's Just the Way It Is

The pike resigned itself to the reality that it can't hunt fish. How many times have you just resigned yourself to a situation, idea or circumstance—sometimes without even thinking about it? Resignation is a lens of belief that plagues society and is the bane of innovation and growth.

How many years did we accept the rigamarole of calling a cab, worrying about the route, and sorting out paying with cash or card because that's just the way it is? Then Uber came along, challenged that complacency and did something about it—making billions of dollars in the process.

Things are the way they are, until you do something about them.

You don't have to have the mind of a pike. Although examining your beliefs might be uncomfortable, an unexamined life is clearly much more painful. (Greek philosopher Socrates didn't even think it was one worth living!) Now reread the three numbered sections on the previous pages. You might find a profound discomfort when you believe you have no control over your future and are stuck with the results that you have. Now you know that even taking the "safe" route and avoiding all discomfort—well, just ask the pike how that turned out.

Discomfort doesn't have to be a bad thing. It makes an excellent starting place for identifying areas where a faulty or limiting belief may be obstructing your perspective. Whenever there is a disconnect between our lens of belief and the result that we want, we feel discomfort. For example, the pike would have felt the discomfort of extreme hunger at a certain point. For us humans, we might feel pain, anxiety or frustration. It's not an evolutionary error or something you need to manage. That discomfort is waving a big flag, signaling that right here is a belief that isn't working for you.

Change Your Lenses, Change Your Results

Another primary way to determine if it is time for new lenses is to check in with your results. Remember how my school grades were being affected by my inability to see the chalkboard clearly? Think about which areas in your life you are not getting the results you want.

Let's say that you can't see the words on this page as clearly as you'd like. Instead of throwing the whole book away, you can simply get a pair of reading glasses to see the page clearly, though this does require facing up to the uncomfortable reality that your vision isn't 20/20. It's the same way in other areas. If you aren't getting the results you want, you don't have to throw out that relationship, business or idea. Instead, you can change your lens of belief.

The CEO of a multibillion-dollar private grocery company, let's call him Joe, approached me a few years ago to work with his company because he was convinced that they weren't able to innovate. "That's just the way it is," he told me. "Our industry just isn't fast to move or try new things."[8]

This company's capabilities and knowledge were impressive: it had operations nailed, marketing was on point, and it had every metric you could imagine to measure and track results. Any suggestions I had for possible areas to innovate were met with answers they already had on hand. It seemed like every sentence out of the leaderships' mouths started with "I know," "I can't" or "That won't work because"—it was as if the entire company had boxed itself in to exactly the results it was getting. There was just no wiggle room. All those metrics and models helped the leadership feel totally justified in their answers, and yet it all started to sound like excuses after a while. Joe and his leadership team were perceiving their business through a belief that knowledge could save them from uncertainty. And they were clinging to it with all their might.

This company was not unusual in this. Many of us are quick to have all the answers, but if you don't have the results you want (over some period, of course), it's time to consider if you too could be peering through a limiting lens of belief.

When the team went through several exercises to identify and let go of some of those limiting beliefs, such as how things "had to go," all of a sudden, brand-new openings for actions and ideas emerged from the team (not from me). What had started as a previously quiet and subdued group transformed into the most talkative crowd imaginable. The energy in the room went from apathetic to electric. In a matter of weeks, several pilots of new ideas were up and running—unheard of in their line of business.

You Get What You Believe

Ever wonder why you can watch two news stations covering the same story but presenting entirely different facts and conclusions? Or go to two investment advisers, show them the same figures, and walk out the door with two completely different investment plans that are "the absolute best way to go"? There's a reason Republicans and Democrats can look at the same world that we all do and draw radically different conclusions—and produce data to prove they're right. It's called confirmation bias. And it's not just done by the media and the politicians; we all do it. It's how our brains work.

Our brain is a little bit like a lazy detective. Once it has a belief in place, it begins to back up that belief by cherry-picking evidence to support it. (And conveniently filtering out evidence that disproves it.) It's hardwired to do this.

Our excuses are often driven by our confirmation bias, because they provide very easy and compelling reasons for something not working out: I didn't have enough time; there wasn't enough money; I'm too old; I'm too young; I don't have the right degree; my boss is out to get me; I don't have the right technology; there's a global pandemic . . . you get the picture. It is far simpler to slap an excuse on something and call it solved than it is to challenge and change a belief. And confirmation bias will make sure that every single example that could be interpreted as something not working out because of whatever excuse you're using will now be collected, labeled and filed away as evidence that this excuse is a fact. And then you wonder why you're stuck.

Here's the thing: you are right. (I said your brain was lazy, not stupid.) You might not have the result you want because of money, time, your age, your boss or any other circumstance, but those things aren't where you can make a difference. Spending time dwelling on those reasons is the biggest hindrance to growth. Ultimately, it's the beliefs you have about those resources, materials, circumstances and so forth that are at play. It's the beliefs you have about what you can do within a certain amount of time. The beliefs you have about what you can do with a certain budget, or what's possible within a pandemic. Tony Robbins, arguably the most popular personal development coach in the world, teaches that it's not an issue with your resources, it's an issue with your resourcefulness!

Those beliefs are powerful. Johns Hopkins professor Curt Richter in the 1950s concluded through an experiment that rats could tread water 240 times longer when they believed they'd be rescued soon compared to when they had no reason to believe this![9] Whether they're working for you or against you, those lenses of belief are massively powerful and will determine your results.

Next time you aren't getting the results you want, instead of grabbing the hall pass of an excuse, try examining your beliefs at a deeper level. When you start to shift your beliefs about yourself and the world around you, expect change.

To quote Henry Ford: "Whether you think you can, or you think you can't—you're right."

Case closed.

Groupthink: Agreement Reality

Up until now, I've been focusing on our individual lenses of reality. But organizations, communities and groups of any kind also confuse absolute reality with their beliefs about reality. The term for this is *agreement reality*. It's usually more difficult to identify because there is homogeneity of thought. But just because we all agree on something, that doesn't make it true. For thousands of years, everyone believed that Earth was at the center of the solar system. It just made sense. People believed they were the highest order of creation, so of course our planet was at the center of it all. Until Nicolaus Copernicus came along in the sixteenth century and radically reoriented our collective view of our place in the universe with his model that showed the Sun at the center of the solar system. Unless you're on the fringe of flat-earthers, you'll agree that the notion of Earth being at the center of the solar system was just a powerful form of agreement reality.

Not only are agreement realities hard to spot, they are hard to challenge because you're going against how those around you view the world. Copernicus provided a proven heliocentric (Sun-centered) model of the solar system, but the early adopters of his model, including Galileo, ended up imprisoned and ostracized for daring to swim against the powerful current of groupthink.

If you're challenging agreement reality—in your family, in your company, or in the world—you can expect to experience some level of ridicule, mockery or even outright harassment. The Wright brothers held the belief that powered flight was possible, and they were famously mocked and ridiculed for their work in aviation by experts and laypersons alike—right up until the time *Kitty Hawk* lifted off and soared into the annals of history.

Just remember, ridicule from others is no concern of yours (we'll return to this subject in greater detail later in the book). Your task is to keep your larger goals in front of you until you take off and soar for yourself.

Change What Works, Leave the Rest

Now that we've explored the origins and nature of our lenses of belief, we'll address in the next chapter how we hunt the discomfort to change these beliefs. Before we do, however, let's ride out with King Arthur's Knights of the Round Table.

As the story goes, King Arthur and his knights saw a vision of the Holy Grail—the cup used by Jesus at the Last Supper that mythically bestows everlasting life and would save the world. Naturally, finding it was high on the knights' priority list, as their land of Camelot was rapidly deteriorating.

On their adventure in finding it, they arrived at a dark wood and decided to split up, each entering the wood alone from what seemed to them the darkest point. Symbolically, they each had to face what scared them the most. Some of the knights would go on to find the Holy Grail, but only after confronting the discomfort of their deepest fears on their particular path.

Facing one's fear is a necessary step for every hero, as noted by famed psychotherapist Carl Jung in *The Structure and Dynamics of the Psyche*. He writes that the hero archetype must be courageous enough to brave intense discomfort in order to find what they value most.[10]

Whether you think of yourself as a hero or not (I'm pretty sure you are), Jung goes on to say, "That which we need the most will be found where we least want to look." The beliefs that will free you from the limiting views of reality are always on the other side of discomfort. They emerge on the other side of the dark wood—inevitably where you least want to look. I'm not suggesting certain beliefs are good or bad, right or wrong, moral or immoral. That's for you to decide. They're simply ways to view things in order to get closer to the results you want.

Because that is the point.

Let me say this loud and clear. I am not suggesting that you should be challenging and changing all your lenses of belief. I'm not sure it's even possible. If you have the results you want, by all means keep all your existing beliefs. The point is to notice when a lens of belief isn't working for you. Notice the discomfort that is arising from this area of your life is out of alignment and then lean into the greater discomfort of dealing with it.

Let's go hunting.

Takeaways

- How you see the world can be inaccurate and limiting.

- Core beliefs drive your thoughts, thoughts drive your actions, actions drive your results.

- You can change your core beliefs if you don't have the results you're looking for; however, doing so can be destabilizing.

- Limiting beliefs may show up as the following statements:
  - I couldn't then, so I can't now.
  - It's not worth the risk.
  - That's just the way it is.

- Because your views and perspectives drive your actions, you will get what you believe.

- Agreement reality can be a form of limiting beliefs held by a group. The beliefs that will free you from the limiting views of reality are always on the other side of discomfort.

CHAPTER 3

Hunting the Discomfort of Reality: Expand Your Reality

Where your fear is, there your task is.

—Carl Jung

I USED TO BE A POWERLIFTER in my younger years. My coach, Steve Stechyshyn, operated a gym out of his garage. Every time I arrived, he'd be playing Guns N' Roses' "Welcome to the Jungle." To this day, whenever I hear that song or catch a whiff of old motor oil, I'm instantly transported back to that garage where I first learned how to push through physical discomfort—and eventually pursue it—in order to get the results I was looking for.

Now, I'm welcoming *you* to the jungle, where I'm going to teach you how to actively hunt discomfort for the results you want. This chapter explores the first practice in the Hunting Discomfort arsenal: expand your reality. We've already covered how your perception of reality is limited by the lenses through which you see the world, and how difficult it is to actually see the lenses that you are looking through. Now I'm going to show you exactly how to spot where your limiting lenses are hiding and what to do once you find them.

Please note that all these practices are dynamic and ongoing. There is no magic wand or silver bullet for creating breakthroughs and growth. If you want to get good at something, what do you do? You gather the knowledge, apply the skills, adjust according to feedback and, as my kindergarten teacher Mrs. Muench would say, "practice, practice, practice." That's exactly what this book was designed to help you do.

Questioning What You See

Do you ever get that gnawing feeling? That irritating mental itch that there's something more? Something *more* for you. But you just don't know exactly what it is?

In *The Matrix*, Neo (played by Keanu Reeves) wakes every day to a similar mental itch. He has a job and some side hustles to get by, a roof over his head, food on the table—a perfectly fine life. And yet, something is gnawing away, eating him from the inside out. It's like he knows there's something else . . .

I won't recount the whole movie; odds are good you know it. (If you don't, go watch it. Right after you finish this book, that is.) Neo's suspicions are confirmed. There is another life, and he is presented with the now infamous choice: The red pill or the blue?

Red pill: The false reality Neo has been living in will be stripped away forever and he will live in a world that is not comfortable, but is real. With this will come the power to make choices that effect real change.

Blue pill: He will be soothed back into dreamlife where everything is a lie, and his life will be safer and more comfortable but ultimately meaningless.

Spoiler alert: Neo chooses the red pill, of course, and they weren't kidding when they said it would be a rude awakening. For a time, his life was a hellscape of discomfort, physically, mentally and emotionally. He was willing to open the door to a small mental itch and found the mother lode of discomfort. Once he adjusted, though, he was unstoppable.

I've always loved this metaphor. You may not be able to pop down to your local pharmacy for the red pill, but you can follow Neo's example to find your way out of your own reality facade. And you do it by being curious and paying attention to the small gnawing areas of discomfort that won't leave you alone. This will lead you directly to the areas in your life where limiting beliefs are distorting your reality. Ignore them and you'll end up interacting with silhouettes of what's real—and wondering why you can't achieve your potential.

To be able to choose the red pill (or anything else) for yourself implies, as Eckhart Tolle notes in his book *The Power of Now*, "consciousness—a high degree of consciousness. Without it, you have no choice."[1] Your first step into this choice is being willing to question if what you're seeing, or how you're seeing it, is real. Perhaps the better way to put it is this: it's the cost of entry—being willing to let go of beliefs that may be false, even if they look real. If you're not, you should put down this book, because the rest of it won't matter.

Closing In—Common Signs of Limiting or False Beliefs

"It's really important to understand we're not seeing reality," said neuroscientist and research professor at Dartmouth College Patrick Cavanagh, talking about his 2019 experiment tracing where conscious perception diverges from physical sensation. "We're seeing a story that's being created for us."[2] Once you are willing to question that story, congratulate yourself—that's a huge first step. You can't locate, challenge or change your beliefs if you are not willing to listen to your discontent to find them—it's like the steady ping of a tracking signal leading you deeper and deeper into uncharted territory. But you will have to employ a few other stalking skills if you want to pinpoint the beliefs that are keeping you from living in an expanded reality. Think of it like being a seasoned tracker who can identify the paw prints of a particular target from the many that are crisscrossing on the jungle floor and then follow them directly to where the prey is hiding.

The following are the most common signs that you may have a hidden faulty or limited belief. Said differently, when your truth isn't the truth. Such beliefs are usually illuminated by some form of cognitive dissonance, or the state of having inconsistent beliefs—often unconscious until we find them:

- **When your feelings don't match your words.** Now that you're listening for your discomfort, why not try to listen to the words coming out of your mouth? Especially the ones that come out automatically. For instance, when someone asks you how you are and you respond with "I'm fine," but you're feeling devastated inside. Or when you say "no problem" to a request, but it is a problem.

  Whenever you notice a disconnect between what you are telling the outside world and how you really feel inside, you're closing in on a faulty or limiting belief.

  To hunt it is to start being honest about how you are doing and feeling. I'm not advocating for inappropriate emotional outbursts, but telling the truth about where you're at, at least with yourself, is the first step out of denial.

- **When you have a negative mood.** Mood is a bit different from feelings. What I'm talking about here is your overall vibe. Does it tend to be more negative or positive?

  Most of us believe that circumstances dictate our mood. For example, if you have a vacation coming up, you might be happy. If your vacation is canceled because you have to work overtime, you might be a little sour.

  Dr. Fernando Flores, from the University of California at Berkeley, writes in his book *Conversations for Action and Collected Essays*, "The unproductive interpretation of moods leads people to focus on the past, to try to blame their bad moods on some recent event." Rather, he continues, "we can interpret moods in terms of assessments that people have about the future."[3] A negative mood, then, might showcase your unwillingness to see the future through a different (and equally valid) lens.

Start with paying attention to your negative mood. Can you start to see what predictions about your future reality you are telling yourself for why you feel this way? Exploring your narrative behind the negative mood is an excellent place to identify a limiting or faulty belief about the world around you and your place in it.

- **When your actions don't line up with your goals.** Okay, you have a lot of goals for yourself: to start a business, get your finances in order, lose weight. Yet you are still in your unful-filling job, your credit card debt continues to climb and your treadmill is collecting dust. What's going wrong? Are you lazy, stupid or undisciplined? Nope, but a powerful (and probably unconscious) limiting belief is preventing you from moving forward in the way that you want.

  Hunting this discomfort means you go beyond merely announcing the goal and pay attention to the inner voice that says "Yeah, but . . . ," giving you an excuse. Unless you unmask the faulty belief, you have no chance of challenging it, and your actions will fail to align with what you say you want in the long term.

- **When you are never wrong (or never right).** Every single person is wrong sometimes. Every single one. If you are someone who prides themselves on being a perfectionist (welcome to the club, by the way) and struggles to accept feedback or others' ideas, is mortified when challenged publicly, always feel you're the most informed, most logical, most experienced—well, I hate to break it to you, but your reality is majorly skewed. This can be a particularly tough limiting belief to get at because the person who is never wrong is never wrong. And, unwilling to take that red pill, will fight tooth and nail to stay blinded. But someone who is never wrong is also someone who will never grow.

If you have even an inkling that this might be you, simply start by admitting that. And start considering where you might be wrong, in an effort to get to the truth (or at least closer to it). By the way, the same idea applies if you generally see yourself as never being right. We'll get to self-doubt soon, but never seeing yourself as having the right answer is just as much of a pitfall as believing you're always right.

- **When you overgeneralize.** Are you an "all or nothing" person? If you're not sure, again, watch your language. Do you use the words *never* and *always* a lot? "The clients will *never* buy that." "My boss is *always* out to get me." Rarely are things all or nothing but usually something in between. Those of us who overgeneralize are working with a limiting belief that protects us from the discomfort of addressing things that may be in our power to change. It's easy to dismiss something when it's always or never, but that dismissal leaves us as powerless victims.

  Your first step to finding this faulty belief is to pay attention to your *always* and *never* statements. Write them down when you hear yourself use them. I'll show you how to transform them in the next section.

- **When you're emotionally triggered.** People, places, things or situations that trigger an immediate negative emotional reaction are like flashing neon signs, indicating that a deep limiting or faulty belief has you in its grips. Emotions are an important part of life, but when they have you—as opposed to you having them—your view of reality is considerably constricted.

  These moments are usually easy to identify. Recall a time in the past when you were triggered. Being triggered can be extremely painful and, just like the core of all these lenses, it's rooted in the past. Being willing to work through it when you're emotionally triggered is going to free your future beyond your wildest imaginings.

- **When you're resigned.** "That's just the way it is." "There's nothing I can do about that." "That's outside my control." Do any of these phrases sound familiar? Resignation is a killer. It kills creativity. It kills dreams. It even killed a pike!

   A lot of things in this world are genuinely out of our control: the pandemic, the weather, the latest happenings on Wall Street. You know what else is out of our control? Everyone else's actions, behaviors and emotions. "There's nothing to be done!" cries your limiting belief.

   Not true. You have control of yourself. You have control of your thoughts, control of your perceptions and control of your response. This is power. And anything else is a limiting belief.

   If you are someone who struggles with resignation, your first step is to pick one thing that you believe you have absolutely no control over. Got it? Good, because we are moving on to our first exercise.

Getting to Know Your Limiting or False Beliefs

I offer quick exercises throughout the book that help you drill down into your life so that you can apply these teachings to your unique journey of hunting discomfort. Most of these exercises are designed to take no more than five minutes, and I highly recommend that you grab a notebook and pen and do them as you move through the book the first time. There is plenty of evidence showing that we are more likely to get around our mental defenses when we dive right in and move quickly. This is not about getting the "right" answer; this is just about being curious. Ready?

1. From this chapter's list of common signs of limiting or false beliefs, identify one of the signs that applies to you.

2. Reread the guidance in that sign's description for flushing the limiting beliefs out into the open so that you can get a good look at them. Take that step for yourself. Quickly jot down a few notes about what you noticed or how you felt doing it.

3. List all the immediate reasons that these beliefs are "true." List all the reasons they may be false. Any yeah-buts coming up? Write them down, too. Seeing your limiting beliefs is the first step to challenging them.

Great job. You're done.

Transforming Limiting Beliefs: Imagine Bigger, Bolder, Beyond Now

We are hunting our limiting beliefs (and all the discomfort this entails) so that we can perceive a more expanded version of reality. Seeing a new reality isn't the result of simply changing our mind about it. Often, our views are defense mechanisms that keep our egos safe by "changing the very facts in [our] mind, so [we] are no longer wrong or culpable," writes psychologist and keynote speaker Guy Winch.[4] We can pay lip service to a new view, but to step into a new reality, we have to experience that new view for ourselves.

Changing beliefs is more powerful than any finite goal. It has resulted in governments, technologies and ideas that have changed history. The founders of the United States believed that something other than a European monarchy was possible (not to mention winning a war with a world power). Reusable rockets to get to space were a pipe dream until the likes of SpaceX, Virgin Galactic and Blue Origin believed otherwise. Even washing our hands wasn't thought to be important until Ignaz Semmelweis, a Hungarian doctor working in Vienna, changed first his and then societies' views on microbes.[5]

But as long as we are limited in our views, we are limited in our ability to imagine transformative results and potential solutions. "The human brain likes simple straight lines," note Bart de Langhe, Stefano Puntoni and Richard Larrick, authors of the *Harvard Business Review* article "Linear Thinking in a Nonlinear World."[6] So we're always trying to fix, adjust and change in linear ways. With that approach, at best what we're going to end up with is a slightly better version of what we already have. Imagining something meaningful, transformative or even exponentially different might seem impossible—at least with your current set of beliefs.

One time while running a workshop, I asked the participants to figure out how they could take a car from New York to Los Angeles in half a day. Try anything I told them. Well, they worked with every bit of knowledge they could muster about the routes between these cities. They consulted maps, considered the speed limits, calculated food, gas and rest stops—there was no way to do it.

There was nothing wrong with their approach, it was just missing something. Something so blatantly obvious that everyone overlooked it. The car. The vehicle they were riding in to get them there. Just like our beliefs, they'd missed the primary driver of all the action.

Well, one person didn't.

The real brainpower in the room. An eight-year-old girl, who was the daughter of one of the participants. She raised her hand and announced with confidence, "It's easy. Just have a car with wings on it."

Some of the more rational-minded adults bristled at the suggestion. Nonsense, cars don't have wings.

But no one had said they had to work only with generally available technology. For this task, they'd only been asked to imagine how to do it.

Only when you start questioning your beliefs and assumptions about what might be possible can you move into more visionary solutions. It requires making room within your preconceived view about yourself or the world for entirely new possibilities to come soaring in, like a winged car, and create breakthrough results.

This workshop exercise is designed to generate creative thinking, and I still sometimes use it in company workshops I run. They're always more fun when kids are involved.

Put Wings on It

Write down a specific goal or dream that you have.

1. What would success look like? Be specific.
2. Write down your assumptions about what it would take to achieve it.
3. Now put wings on that car. List three mind-boggling, ridiculously over-the-top fantasy ways of achieving that goal or dream. (Have some fun here: let go of limits for just a moment and fly.)

How to Hack Facts

Flying cars aren't generally available at your local Range Rover dealership. (Airplanes are relatively easy to come by though—they were once a ridiculous notion as well.) I am not proposing that you set goals using the imaginary resources of an eight-year-old, but I am suggesting that we are so overly committed to the "sure thing" that we are wildly limiting our understanding of what results are possible.

Let's talk about the "sure thing," i.e., facts and data.

Data never lies, they say. It's true, but how the data is presented, what data is presented or how the data is interpreted certainly *can* lie. We talk about facts like they are the indisputable truth, and yet these days it seems that people can come up with whatever "facts" they need to bolster whatever position they have. With so much conflicting information out there, how can you trust anything?

There's a good test for this. It's called physics.

I have a friend who works for a big technology company worth billions on the stock exchange and has a reputation of getting things done. The CEO approached him one day and asked to have an entire data center up and running in a new location within one week. You don't have to be a tech expert to know that that's a short amount of time for a big project. My friend pushed back on the schedule, resources and funds . . . but he wasn't permitted to finish his list of "why we can't." The CEO cut him off and simply gave him the physics test.

"Do the laws of physics make it impossible to do?" he asked my friend. "Or just your beliefs about what can or cannot be done?"

That data center was built in one week. It was a herculean effort that squeezed every last drop of creativity, time and resources from the team, but they did it.

When you're looking to see if in reality something is truly possible or not, use that same test. If physics renders it impossible, it's impossible (unless you're Neo). If you can't explain it away with the laws of physics, it *is* technically possible. And it's up to your potential, creativity and resourcefulness to figure it out.

Is It Physically Possible?

Let's go back to that goal or dream you named in the previous exercise. You now know what success looks like, but how do you get there?

1. List reasons you haven't yet realized that goal.
2. Are those reasons backed up by physics? Or just by relationships, money, time or any other excuse?

If physics doesn't stop you . . .

3. What would someone you admire do to achieve the goal?
4. What might you now do to achieve the goal?

When Feelings Masquerade as Facts

When I first began public speaking, my fear was real. Gearing up to that big breakthrough moment in Singapore involved a lot of practicing. First in front of my sister. And then in front of small audiences, where I continually froze up, started stuttering or forgot my words completely. I was scared, anxious, insecure and usually a bit angry at myself for both messing up and not naturally being better. Sounds fun, right? Once these emotions were triggered, all the negative thoughts started as well: *I'll never be able to do this. Everyone must think I'm an idiot. Why bother? There is no point.*

Here's the thing. If you are going to push yourself into areas that make you uncomfortable, at some point negative thoughts will try to take over, and they'll bring all those unpleasant emotions with them. These thoughts are generated by your limiting beliefs, and that's why when your emotions are triggered like that, your view of reality is almost certainly obscured.

At certain points, that's unavoidable. Welcome to being human. Just know that whatever is happening during that emotional time may look different from what is happening in reality. The good news is that this unpleasant experience offers a golden opportunity to dig in and unearth where you can begin to expand your current view of reality.

What to Do Instead

Emotions are not the problem—hanging onto them is. A qualitative study of Norwegian Healthy Life Centre participants found that people "described being burdened by an emotional baggage with problems from childhood and/or with family, work and social life issues" when trying to change to a healthier diet.[7] They felt that emotional baggage left them "unable to act in accordance with the health knowledge they possessed"! I use an exclamation mark because it once again shows that knowledge alone doesn't work.

Hanging on to emotions will block your view of what's real and possible every time. It's important to feel and move through the feelings to let them go and not be limited by them. The following exercise will help you get in touch with some of your stuck feelings so that you can fully feel them and then challenge the story that's giving you those feelings.

Freedom from Feelings

You may wish to do this exercise in a quiet and private place. Give yourself at least five minutes to do it.

1. When was the last time you were triggered with a negative emotion? (Anger, grief, fear, rejected, resentful, insecure, inadequate . . . you get the idea.) Write out the scenario, being as specific as possible about the emotions you were feeling. Write them all down.

2. As you write, welcome back those feelings and let them move through you—yell, cry, laugh, no judgment—at least if you're doing it in private. Whatever shows up is whatever shows up. Take the time you need; don't rush these emotions. If you don't resist having them, they will move through you and leave on their own accord.

3. Now write down what beliefs or views you think you have that caused that reaction.

4. Examine those views. Are any worth challenging? Write down a new belief that is more expansive. For example, replace "I'm not good at public speaking" with "I will master public speaking with practice."

5. Now tack your new-belief statement on the wall where you can see it. Time to start living it.

Get Unstuck from the Muck

I want to focus for a moment on the particular challenge of feeling absolutely stuck. I'm talking about the kind of stuck where you feel hopeless about change. Maybe you're stuck with a board of directors you don't like, you're stuck in difficult relationships, you hate where you live or you're imprisoned by obligations you simply can't get out of. We all have instances like this, and you already know that it's not just a matter of flipping a switch and changing your view. Especially if you're new to this whole paradigm-shifting thing.

But trust me, this is no different from any other perceived problem you have. When you're stuck—in one area or in every area—it really is just an inaccurate view of reality that you're dealing with. I know, it seems so real, right? But that place of stuck-ness isn't a sign that you're trapped; it's a sign that it's time to make a change.

What to Do Instead of Being Stuck: Part 1

I have a hands-down favorite way of breaking the logjam of being stuck. It can be fun, albeit challenging. Actually, challenging is the exact point.

Do something really hard.

Whenever you do something that's not easy for you, you demonstrate an expanded view of what's possible for yourself. In other words, you expand your view of reality. This is not an intellectual exercise, this is physical. I'm talking about putting yourself out there and blasting through, in a very tangible way, the limiting belief of what you are capable of.

A few times a year I host #NoMatterWhat adventures for those looking to actively hunt discomfort in order to break through their perceived barriers. These are trips to different parts of the world to accomplish feats that seem scary, impossible, physically demanding or maybe just entirely new. We've scuba-dived the Catalina Islands, cycled to the top of Mount Evans (the highest paved road in the United States) and sailed the Galápagos Islands.

These adventures are designed to disrupt and break one's status quo in order to provide a new vista. Inevitably, participants break through their personal deadlocks because they are no longer confined to their typical limited view.

You don't have to cross the world to disrupt your personal status quo. You could sign up for a marathon, a dance class, a yoga membership, it doesn't really matter what as long as it's something that's physically hard for you. When you step outside the safety of your comfort zone, enjoy the new view. Watch your world and your potential enlarge every time you do this. Enjoy the new you.

Put It into Action

Book yourself an adventure—big or small—right now. A new fitness class, a long run, a Tough Mudder or something else that pushes your edges. Feel free to start small. But I recommend at some moment doing something that pushes you to your breaking (breakthrough) point. Message me if you need help. (You'll find my contact info at SterlingHawkins.com.)

By the way, knowing you might be able to run a marathon (or anything else) is no substitute for actually doing it.

What to Do Instead of Being Stuck: Part 2

There's another way to expand your reality in order to move through a stuck area of your life. For this one, you're going to need the help of others.

Let's imagine you and me are sitting across from each other at a table. Between us is this book—upright, with the front cover facing you. What would happen if we both described it?

From my vantage point, I'd see testimonials and a bio. From your perspective, you'd see the cover art. Both of our views would be accurate, just incomplete. If we invited more people to the table, we'd discover even more perspectives on this book.

You can tackle the stuck areas in your life in the exact same way. You're not going to be looking at this book, but you can gather several people to look at the situation you are facing. When you have multiple people looking at the same thing, it becomes much easier to perceive how different perspectives might also be true. Just like viewing this book from different angles, you could all be looking at the same thing but needing each other's vantage points for a more complete view.

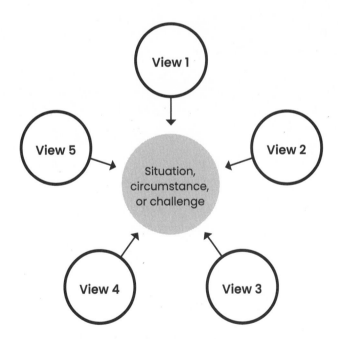

Figure 3.1: Perspectives Widen Your View of Reality. Having various people view a situation you're feeling stuck in will give you perspectives beyond what you could ever see yourself.

Don't avoid healthy conflict in this exercise, by the way. The discomfort of discussing (not fighting about) the points you disagree on is exactly—and I mean *exactly*—where you'll find the freedom from getting unstuck. Before you begin, be sure to have consensus that you are all committed to taking the time and space to explore the hard conversations in order to get closer to the truth.

When you find yourself vehemently disagreeing with someone's point of view, do yourself a favor and start looking at how that other person might be right. If you had their same beliefs, perspective, experiences and ethics, chances are you'd have the same opinion they have. It's not an opportunity to block, antagonize or ignore. It's an opportunity for you both to get closer to an expanded view of reality.

Gather the Group

Invite three to six people to join you to discuss a particular area (professional or personal) where you are feeling stuck. Ideally, these are individuals whose worldviews are not identical to yours but whose opinions you trust.

1. Present the stuck area. Do not take more than five minutes for this.
2. Attain consensus that tough and honest feedback is valuable and everyone is willing to stick with the exercise, even if it gets uncomfortable.
3. Ask each person for their thoughts, advice and perspective on why you're stuck.
4. Actively work to see things from their point of view. Remember, rejecting their thoughts before truly hearing them will keep you exactly where you are: stuck.

Warning: A typical response to feeling stuck is wanting to redouble your efforts—90 percent of what I see on Instagram is about how hard work is the only thing between you and a successful outcome. Wrong. In *Get Your Brain Unstuck*, Ron Friedman writes, "Research tells us something different. While grit does have its role[, . . .] dogged persistence can actually backfire."[8] It turns out that when you're stuck, simply "more focus" will result only in a narrower view.

How to Know When You're on the Right Track

You'll know that hunting the discomfort of expanding your reality is working when . . . drumroll here . . . you start getting results! It's that simple. It might not be immediate (though it could be), but over time your goals will start lining up better with your results. This is the number one indicator of your success. Others include:

- **You feel alive.** Moving through discomfort will typically leave you feeling rejuvenated, exhilarated and more alive than you've felt in some time. Deep down, you've always known the potential you have. When you lose the limiting beliefs that are holding you back, you are essentially unleashing this part of yourself.

- **You face headwinds from the status quo.** People at your job, in your community and even your friends and family know only a limited version of who you are. As you hunt down and change your limited and faulty lenses on the world, your words, actions, ideas and self will begin to change. Your vehicle with wings! Expect pushback. Understand that who you are may also be threatening the comfort zone of those around you. Know that pushback means the process is working. (And you can always gift them a copy of this book to get them on board.)

- **You see the world differently.** Expanding your reality shifts how you see yourself, others and the world. Maybe the view will be a little different, maybe it will be radically different. You won't have to force it, it will just happen naturally because your vantage point has changed.

- **Your discomfort changes.** Once you start actively hunting discomfort, the experience of the discomfort will change. Things that used to trigger you may no longer. Emotions that took over might not be there anymore. It takes time, but discomfort isn't static—it can and will change, and when it does, it means you're doing it right.

Here's to a New Reality

Your unexamined beliefs about yourself and the world will *always* limit you. Until you make the unconscious conscious, it will direct your life and you will call it fate, as the late psychologist Carl Jung suggested.[9]

If you don't have the results you want, now is the perfect time to question the beliefs you have in order to expand your view of what might be possible. Remember, there's not just one better way to view things. More better ways will naturally present themselves as you take steps forward. You'll get better at doing it, too. Everything you want is on the other side of discomfort: you just have to be courageous enough to push through. The way out is through—through the discomfort of facing reality.

Takeaways

- We are all limited in our views of what's possible, but by questioning your beliefs and assumptions, you can start to shift your view.

- You are operating from limiting or faulty beliefs when

  - Your feelings don't match your words.
  - You have a negative mood.
  - Your actions don't line up with your goals.
  - You are never wrong (or never right).
  - You overgeneralize.
  - You are emotionally triggered.
  - You are resigned.

- Data, or more likely the interpretation of data, can be misleading. Especially when groups of people buy into it. Only the laws of physics dictate what's possible or not; use them as a rule.

- Feelings can seem like facts. They are not. You must go through the feeling to get to the real nature of things.

- To get unstuck you can (1) do something that is challenging and outside your comfort zone or (2) gather people to understand different perspectives.

- Hard work alone won't get you unstuck. You must move through your discomforts.

- Hunting the discomfort of reality is working when

  - You have results!
  - You feel alive.
  - You genuinely see the world differently.
  - Your discomfort changes—it no longer is where it once was.

- The way out of faulty or limiting beliefs is through the discomfort of expanding your view of reality.

CHAPTER 4

Discomfort #2: Self-Doubt

Doubt kills more dreams than failure will.

—**Suzy Kassem**

Ludwig van Beethoven is not your typical poster boy for self-doubt. His legacy is one of rising above the limitations of deafness to create music that resonates with power, confidence and triumph throughout the ages. And yet, the world almost missed the gift of much of his music when the great composer lapsed into lethargy and a lengthy depression that coincided with his darkest period of self-doubt in his personal life. But this connection between self-doubt and creative drought was only understood after his death.

His assistant, when cleaning out his desk, found a secret cache of letters written to his "Immortal Beloved."[1] For the longest unproductive musical period in Beethoven's adult life, he had been pouring his inspiration and emotions onto these pages and not composing musical scores. And he didn't even send these letters. He could release his music to the world, but not his love. In this area of his life, Beethoven was tormented by self-doubt. He never gave his beloved a chance to love him back, and he died unmarried, his romantic love unrequited. But thankfully, he did get back to composing.

We'll never know how many masterpieces never came into being while Beethoven was mired in self-doubt about a relationship, but we can learn this from the eminent maestro—self-doubt is a very human condition, and it plagues even the greatest among us. Unaddressed, it's a dream killer, and that's why in this chapter we are setting our sights on hunting self-doubt.

Self-doubt is the no-man's-land of indecision between belief and disbelief. You know the feeling: mentally wrestling with questions and insecurities. This is often accompanied by a visceral sense that something terrible is going to happen, which sends adrenaline coursing through your body. When in the grips of self-doubt, you can feel utterly powerless. And if you don't address the discomfort of self-doubt, it can act like a self-fulfilling prophecy, causing you to retreat from your goals and dreams before you really give them a fair chance. I get it, it's natural to not want to spend time on something that's not guaranteed to work out, but if you let self-doubt call the shots, you are essentially guaranteeing those results.

The romantic tragedy in Beethoven's life is paralleled in one way or another in all of us. Maybe your self-doubt is focused on worrying that you don't know enough about the new business idea you have, so you never start it. Or it's a plaguing insecurity that you've made the wrong choice in something, so shy away from making any other choices. Or maybe you suffer from anxiety about the potential embarrassment of publicly going after a goal and failing.

That's the thing: self-doubt knows when the stakes are high—that's why it shows up to kill our dreams, not our passing fancies. It feels like self-protection because it challenges our identity, but it is actually the opposite. Self-doubt feeds on fear and will devour all our ambition if we let it.

We may never know the details of who Beethoven loved so deeply, but we know our own passions, our own goals and our own dreams. We can hold on to them as regrets on our deathbed, or we can hunt the discomfort of self-doubt and do something about it.

Needless to say, hunting this discomfort is not, well, comfortable.

It's easier to wake up in the familiar world of self-doubt that 99 percent of people wake up in. A world of "I want . . . ," "I wish . . . ," "I hope . . . ," "I could try . . . ," "I might . . ." and even "I can't . . ."

Have you noticed how many times a day you utter those words?

I want to hit my performance target . . .

I wish we had some investors . . .

I hope I can retire early . . .

I could try to learn that new program . . .

I might ask for a promotion . . .

I can't possibly say *that* . . .

Consistently expressing noncommittal statements like this is a tell-tale sign that you are dealing with self-doubt. When we frame something as existing in the realm of only a *possibility*, we're avoiding the discomfort of being responsible for making something work out no matter what.

Another telltale sign is a pattern of *self-sabotage*—killing your important projects, relationships or business ideas before they have a chance to fail. You may be eliminating the discomfort of not knowing how things will turn out. But it's temporary relief that will leave you without any new results.

Or perhaps you are the person who *convinces yourself* that you don't want a particular result to begin with, in order to avoid the discomfort entirely. But pretending something that isn't true makes you the hunted. You'll never shake the ache of unfulfilled dreams.

Yet another telltale sign of a self-doubter is someone who loves to *reason their way out* of something. Instead of facing their inner insecurity, they scour their external environment for faults, problems, evidence or blame for why they can't move forward. Waiting for the perfect market conditions, the perfect age, the perfect amount of money only leaves you waiting, with the same old results you've always had. Maybe you've noticed by now that self-doubt is a form of not seeing the reality about yourself clearly.

But the number one telltale sign that you've got a serious problem with self-doubt is that you struggle with commitment.

Choose Your Own Adventure, but You Have to Choose

I used to love those "choose your own adventure" books as a kid. Every few pages I would be left with several choices, each leading to one of many different possible endings. But whenever I was faced with a choice—a turning point in the story—I kept my finger on that spot in the book, so if I didn't like where I ended up, I could always go back.

The ironic thing is that I rarely finished any of those books. After a few chapters, it became so unwieldy and confusing as I tried to keep track of all my nondecisions that I just threw in the towel. There were just too many options!

"When you fail to commit to a path, indecision becomes your decision." I've heard this from nearly every coach I've ever had. I've heard this fear of commitment framed as "keeping options open," but too many options are more likely to lead to overwhelm and paralysis than to clarity and action.

Maybe you are someone who prides themselves on waiting for just the right data points or other measures of definitive proof to guide your direction—even though we all know there are still countless stories that exemplify the dangers of this way of thinking.

Don't Be Kodak and Fail to Try

Steven Sasson is the inventor of the digital camera. While working for Kodak in the 1970s, he made history when he created and then patented the process for the first digital images.

"It was only my persistence that drove this innovation," Sasson shared when I interviewed him.[2] "I had to sneak parts out of the trash, borrow parts from the assembly and build the digital camera one circuit at a time." Management didn't stop him, but they didn't support him either. "I'd share every advancement I was making to management time and time again. The consensus was that I should keep working on it. However, I got the feeling that they hoped the project would prove unsuccessful."

When he was successful, however, the organizational leaders were more concerned with their list of unknowns. They were worried that the image quality of digital wasn't at the same resolution as print and that the idea would therefore fail. They worried that changing customer perceptions would hurt Kodak if the company got into digital. They couldn't project digital sales—would they lose the complementary impulse business that came with people forced to go into retail stores to first drop off their film and then pick it up when it was printed? Ultimately, they feared that their profit from digital cameras would be nothing close to that from the traditional camera business. Afterall, Kodak had a flourishing print business that was hugely lucrative. How could they possibly replace that?

So, they decided to keep their options open until there was some evidence to guide their decision. They waited and waited until it was too late. Fuji, Nikon, Casio and others went to market, and the digital camera business quickly cannibalized traditional cameras. According to Sasson, "There wasn't anything that could be done. Kodak just wasn't ready." In January 2012, Kodak filed for bankruptcy.

Keeping your options open is an illusion driven by self-doubt. The world won't stand still for you while you worry, wait and watch. If you never play your cards in a poker game, eventually the mandatory blind bets will leave you bankrupt. The world changes, your business changes and you change, too. Or maybe you don't, and you end up like Kodak.

The Stats Might Be Lion

Seeing lions on the African savanna has been a highlight of my many adventures. I caught only a glimpse of a pride at rest, and even then I was struck by their size and power. Seeing them lounging with each other outside the confines of a zoo was awe-inspiring. Whether you've seen a lion in the wild, in captivity, or on TV, odds are good that you know you don't want to come face to face with a hungry one. Their prowess as hunters is legendary.

As notorious as they are, their proficiency at hunting might not be as great as you think. According to Alert, a nonprofit organization dedicated to African lion conservation, lions are successful in hunts only about 30 percent of the time.[3] That means that 70 percent or more of the time they fail.

Just let that sink in for a moment. That's a 70 percent failure rate for the thing they are known for doing best.

Now think about one of your past failures. Maybe you failed in an important presentation or in a relationship or in anything else that mattered to you. Odds are good that this particular instance of failure fed into some self-doubt. That self-doubt told you that a failure in the future is more likely. And each subsequent failure proves to you that you're right. (Remember confirmation bias? Well, that's one of self-doubt's favorite tools.)

Let's take it one step further. Let's say you have a failure rate of 70 percent. That means 70 percent of potential clients reject you out of the gate, 70 percent of presentations are rated as a zero out of ten, 70 percent of your research papers are rejected, 70 percent of your investment inquiries are turned down—how might you experience that? Imagine the kind of things you'd say to yourself about it. If you're like many people and companies I work with, a failure of something important (even at a much lower rate than 70 percent) leads to doubts that sound like: "I'm not cut out for this." "Maybe I'm in the wrong profession." "Maybe we're in the wrong market." "Our competitors must know something we don't." "I'm going to go home, order a pizza and watch a movie until I feel better, and likely never try again."

That's the difference between people and lions. For a lion, a failed hunt is just a failed hunt. There's no voice of self-doubt telling them that they're not cut out for the job of hunting. You don't see lions sitting around sharing about their inadequacies, inabilities or crushing doubts. They simply keep hunting.

Remember, it's never *ever* your past failure that creates and feeds self-doubt. It's your interpretation of your past experience of failure.

The Benefit of Self-Doubt

Self-doubt isn't all bad. If you don't heed the cautions of self-doubt from time to time, there can be some very serious and very real consequences.

Imagine if you never paused to question your actions, direction or thinking. Blind and baseless overconfidence is the opposite of self-doubt—and is an equally destructive way of being in the world. (Arguably *more* destructive, since making decisions when you haven't put in the thought or care can be dangerous to others as well as to yourself.) Healthy self-doubt, on the other hand, as psychologist and writer Barbara Markway notes, promotes planning, preparation, self-reflection and engaging with others to determine the most effective way possible to create the best result.[4]

Healthy self-doubt means we can see and articulate our limitations. That's the first step to overcoming them. Your nagging self-doubt may be a sign that there's a danger ahead and more information is needed. Or that it's time to ask for help. When you can be open about your self-doubt, you can have more straightforward and honest conversations that actually make a difference.

Take comfort in the fact that everyone has self-doubt. Pretending otherwise and trying to cover up self-doubt with bravado makes it worse. Here's the thing: without some amount of fear and self-doubt to overcome, you'll never have a chance to build your courage and confidence. Without self-doubt, there could be no growth, because there's nothing to grow from. Doubt forces us to look at other alternatives that may work better. Self-doubt can be a gift, especially once we realize it isn't showing us what we're not capable of, it's showing us what we care about the most. Seen in this way, self-doubt can be shining light down the path to our greatest success.

Self-Doubt Can Be a Path

When I look back to that time in my life when I was riddled with self-doubt, I see such a path. I knew public speaking was critical to my future if I was going to achieve any level of success, and I committed to it in a big way by securing that speech in Singapore. I desperately wanted this skill, and my crippling self-doubt illuminated a path I hadn't seen before. It was a path of study, preparation and practice to address this inability. In other words, self-doubt showed me what I had to learn next. And I knew that if I wanted to move forward on this path, I was going to have to work for it.

I started by looking up local Toastmasters clubs. (Toastmasters is a global network of clubs for people who want to practice public speaking.) The first time I visited, I sat quietly at the back of the room and slipped out at the end of the meeting, relieved I'd not been called on to talk. I visited another club and did the same. I just didn't have the courage to raise my hand and speak up—the self-doubt was still too great. But I was putting myself in the environment to make a change.

I had my breakthrough moment at my third Toastmasters club, finally getting up to stumble, bumble and flounder through speaking to a small group of people. I had taken the first step. One foot in front of the other, I walked the path. (The Toastmaster members in the room that day, including Yvette Frontera, Ascanio Pignatelli, Hartmut

Eggert, Archie Hill and Gavin Masumiya, would change my life first by listening to me and then by coaching me in true Toastmasters style over time.)

One speech after the other, I again took a page from my kindergarten teacher and practiced, practiced and practiced—in total hundreds, if not thousands, of times. I would study, write a speech, build some slides, only to throw the whole thing out and start again. I intuitively knew it was a discomfort to move through, not to get stopped by. And when the day finally came and I stepped onto the stage in Singapore . . . well, you know the story already.

Without that self-doubt driving me, I never would have put in so much work and effort. I likely would have given a fine presentation, only to fly home to about the same life I was living. Instead, self-doubt created a path that launched an entirely new career. I awakened to a new possibility in my life that I was good at, and I loved. Without overcoming my self-doubt, I would have lived a life without that discovery. Self-doubt drove me to learn the skills so that my confidence, when it did come, was based on hard work, experience and practice. And that's the kind of confidence that can change anything.

Commitment Changes Your Brain

There's a small but important part of your brain called the reticular activating system (RAS) that does for your brain what a bouncer does for a club. Just like a bouncer keeps out unwanted clientele, the RAS filters out all the unnecessary information between you and what you need. It's your super-focuser. It's why if, in a busy conference space with people, displays, music, lighting, someone calls out your name, you immediately pick it out of the din. Or why, when you buy a car, you suddenly see that car everywhere. The RAS takes what you're focused on and creates a filter so those things in your focus are presented to your conscious mind.

When your RAS meets the confirmation bias of self-doubt (that is picking out patterns of failure in order to predict future failure), you end up caught in the powerful current of these combined forces. Self-doubt trains your RAS to look for reasons, justifications, excuses and distractions to keep you from achieving what it is you want to achieve. Your focus will hone in on why you cannot do it. Down, down, down you spiral.

Good news: that spiral works both ways. Instead of being flushed down into the spiral of self-doubt, you can create an upward spiral of growth. Not by snapping your fingers but by building confidence. Confidence is built one commitment at a time. Make a commitment, achieve it, acknowledge it, repeat. If you don't achieve it, acknowledge it, learn from it, repeat. According to Albert Bandura, Stanford professor of psychology, as you do this, you'll build higher self-efficacy by showing yourself a greater likelihood of future success.[5] You'll begin cultivating a belief in your ability to figure things out no matter the circumstances. Best of all, your RAS will kick in and create a filter that focuses on pathways, shortcuts and resources to achieve your stated goal.

In the next chapter we are going to go hunting for areas of self-doubt and examine how your self-doubt is showing you where to locate the greatest potential gains for your life or business. Most importantly, we are going to learn how to push through the discomfort of commitment and harness it in order to drive breakthroughs and results you may not have even thought possible.

Takeaways

- Self-doubt is the fastest way to kill your dreams.

- Indecision (keeping options open) can be paralyzing over time as more options accumulate.

- Past failure doesn't create self-doubt; your interpretation of it does.

- Self-doubt can show you what you really care about.

- Your brain is tuned to pick patterns of failure if you let it.

- Commitment moves you forward to retune your brain to look for paths to success.

CHAPTER 5

Hunting the Discomfort of Self-Doubt: Get a Tattoo

The most important moments are the ones that make you realize there's no turning back. You've crossed a line, and you're stuck on the other side now.

—Tokyo, in "Pasodoble," *Money Heist*

US PRESIDENT JOHN F. KENNEDY took the stage at Rice University on September 12, 1962, and committed to one of the most audacious things anyone had ever heard. He announced to the entire world, "We choose to go to the Moon. We choose to go to the Moon in this decade and do the other things, not because they are easy but because they are hard."

It is important to note that at the time, neither President Kennedy nor the brightest and best at NASA knew exactly how we were going to reach the Moon. But Kennedy knew that commitment was an antidote to self-doubt and a shortcut to results. He also knew that a public declaration of a bold commitment would inspire the nation and drive ingenuity, creativity and determination like never seen before. Within the decade, Neil Armstrong took the one giant leap for mankind on the surface of the Moon.

When I teach the most decisive way to break free from the stranglehold of self-doubt, I talk about Getting a Tattoo. I'm not talking about ink on your body. Rather, it's a metaphor for a way of operating in the world. Getting a Tattoo is committing in a way where there's no safety net, no contingency, no plan B. When faced with no options, people tend to overcome. Something the explorer Hernán Cortés knew when he burned his ships on an Americas expedition back in 1519 (he actually intentionally sank them, but you get the idea).[1] Those who have had the largest impact on the world have gone all-in.

We are going to look at exactly how to commit at the level of Getting a Tattoo, including how to choose what you are committing to in the first place. But we begin our hunt as we did last time, with identifying the areas where self-doubt may be hiding.

The Telltale Signs of Self-Doubt

Self-doubt is insidious. It operates undercover, sneaking its way into your life, all the while whispering that it is protecting you and keeping you safe. It grows bigger and bigger while shrinking your world ever smaller. That's because self-doubt is highly risk averse. But we all know that if you take all the risk out of life, you take the life out of living.

We touched on some of the telltale signs of self-doubt in the previous chapter, but now we're going deeper so you can hunt those that are relevant for you. To hunt down your self-doubt, you have to first identify what it looks like, sounds like and feels like in the wild. Luckily for us, self-doubt has some dead giveaways.

Telltale Sign 1: You Use Noncommittal Language

Imagine a US president taking the oath of office and saying, "I *hope* to faithfully execute the Office of President of the United States."

Or a wedding ceremony where the officiant asks the couple if they take each other for richer or poorer, in sickness and health . . . and they say, "I'll *try*."

What about receiving an acceptance letter from your dream university that reads: "Congratulations. You *might* be admitted to . . ."

Wishing and hoping is language best saved for wells and birthday cakes.

Since it's sometimes difficult to notice your thoughts, start with listening for the instances in which this noncommittal language comes out of your mouth: *could, try, might, can't*. This is oftentimes self-doubt.

Richard Condon, one of my mentors and a world-renowned business coach who has trained thousands all over the world, says, "You don't have to commit to anything to hope."[2] And as we saw in the previous chapter, without commitment you can't build any kind of credible self-belief.

Telltale Sign 2: You Focus on Your Perceived Flaws

Everyone has negative thoughts and self-talk. But if it is one of your predominant characteristics, that's a sign that self-doubt is taking over and likely working in tandem with your RAS to magnify negative perspectives and ignore the positive ones. This may look like:

- Ignoring all praise or positive feedback, and obsessing over anything that indicates you didn't perform perfectly.
- Blaming yourself for everything, even if it has nothing to do with you.
- Predicting that future events will likely have negative outcomes for personal reasons, for example, walking out of a sales meeting thinking "I'll never get that deal!"
- Evaluating yourself—and often the world—around you through extreme dichotomies of right or wrong. If something you did wasn't 100 percent your best performance, you must be bad and wrong. (I know this one especially well.)

Lisa W. Coyne, a senior clinical consultant at McLean Hospital's Child and Adolescent OCD Institute, when talking about focusing on our self-critical voice, said that "people run into trouble when they get stuck listening to their mind solely, rather than being out in the world and noticing that sometimes the mind isn't correct about what it thinks."[3] By overly focusing on how you are always the problem (rather than on how you can improve), you blind yourself to the inner and external resources available to you. This can be a very damaging form of self-protection to be living with (instead of hunting), but ultimately, that is all it is, a defense mechanism.

Telltale Sign 3: It's Easier to Imagine Failure Than Success

I did my undergrad at Bentley University, a great business school right outside Boston. Whenever I was given an assignment, I would immediately start thinking about backup plans in case I couldn't get it done. I could skip class the day it was due to avoid the embarrassment of not turning in the assignment. I could have a computer meltdown that "accidentally" deleted my work. I could talk to the teacher about an extension. For some reason, all these alternatives were far easier to imagine than just getting the project done.

I know now this was because of self-doubt. This kind of focus on alternatives, backup plans and safety nets rather than just getting to work is a big waving red flag, signaling that self-doubt is present. There's a time and place for safety nets—just ask my financial adviser—but not at the expense of distracting your focus from what it will take to succeed.

Telltale Sign 4: You Avoid Making Plans Too Far in Advance

When I first started speaking professionally, I had no idea that event organizers must plan as much as eighteen months—a year and a half—ahead of the actual event. They're locking in event spaces, confirming the speakers, working out food and tech logistics and much more.

In the past, I would plan no more than six months into the future. Even then, I only really paid attention to my immediate plans. I couldn't focus until it was just around the corner. That changed when serious offers for large speaking engagements began rolling in, demanding that I commit to sometimes a year or more into the future. At first I resisted: How did I know what I would be doing in eighteen months? I could be anywhere in the world, doing something much more interesting—Did I really want to lock myself in? And then I caught it. This was just another guise of self-doubt rearing its head and balking at commitment. I realized I had the capacity to figure it out when the time came!

Maybe this is you, too. Perhaps you don't like to make plans sooner than the night of. You like to see how you feel, or leave your schedule open in case something better comes along. There's nothing wrong with that, but there's also no growth. Always having an out will lure you back to your comfort zone just as things are getting hard and you are on the verge of a breakthrough. You can live your life figuring out your next step depending on what happens, or you can live knowing that no matter what happens, you can figure it out.

Telltale Sign 5: You Avoid Serious Conversations about Your Commitments

Ever ghosted someone? Apparently it's a dating trend these days. It's when you abruptly cut off contact with someone without any kind of explanation or warning. Any attempts to reach you are met with silence. Ghosting is a toxic habit that's not limited to the singles scene. Let's say you are someone who does everything in your power to avoid legal contracts or tough HR conversations. Or maybe you're someone who doesn't respond to emails from people you know. Guess what? That's also ghosting, just in a different way. Of course, being "busy" is just an excuse.

If you are a chronic avoider of certain conversations—be it business or personal—you've got a problem with commitment and therefore a problem with self-doubt.

Moving toward real commitment requires discussion, openness and addressing questions that—you guessed it—make you feel uncomfortable.   .

Telltale Sign 6: You Have Many Casual Relationships but No Close Ones

Self-doubt thrives in social isolation. It will do everything in its power to convince you that it is preferable, to avoid being vulnerable in all your relationships. If people don't know you, they can't reject the real you. Right?

Pay attention. If you're someone who has no (or very few) close relationships in your life, your closest relationship is likely with self-doubt.

"You have to try to help people understand and accept you, which conversely means you have to understand and accept yourself," says Donald Miller, author of the *New York Times* bestseller *Scary Close: Dropping the Act and Finding True Intimacy*.[4] Building long-term relationships requires a willingness to be vulnerable. You know what else they require? Commitment. (You starting to notice a pattern here?) You must be accountable in order to build trust with others. One of the most important ways to build trust is to follow through on your commitments—doing what you said you would do and, if not, addressing that with integrity.

Telltale Sign 7: You're Too Picky about Conditions under Which You'll Commit

"Mercury is in retrograde!" the yoga instructor yelled at me when I had the audacity to ask her if she knew next week's class schedule.

I was new in Los Angeles and going "full West Coast"—according to my East Coast friends—by getting into yoga. But this independent studio owner didn't want to commit to class schedules because of some astrological phenomenon. (A very serious one, I've been told by many.)

Whether Mercury is in retrograde, it's Friday the 13th, your personal life is a mess, you're too busy or not busy enough—there will always be conditions that aren't perfect for you to commit to something. Being too picky about the circumstances under which you will commit is a sign you're doubting your own ability to deliver. And maybe even looking for reasons to avoid it.

Telltale Sign 8: You Equate Commitment with Losing Your Freedom

Recently, I spoke at a Denver entrepreneurship group. When I asked the attendees about their goals, an overwhelming number of them said "freedom." But when we drilled deeper, what they really meant was they didn't want to commit to anything. Ever. They wanted to do what they wanted, when they wanted, with whom they wanted. Because who wants limits, right? Wrong.

As someone who helps others break free from their limiting beliefs, I found this especially interesting. Here was a group of people who already believed that they operated outside of limiting beliefs—all they wanted was to be free from the shackles of limits, a world without rules and commitments.

But this too is a form of self-doubt, dressed up in one of its sneakiest guises.

I invited the participants to play a game. After dividing them into teams, I pointed to one team and instructed, "You go first." There was silence, so I asked if there were any questions. You can probably guess what they were . . .

"What game are we playing?"

"What are the rules?"

"Are we in teams?"

"What are my options?"

Even the simplest game needs some sort of communal agreement, whether spoken or implied—how turns are taken, what's fair and unfair, how do you win—before we can play.

It's the same in anything. Limitless options might sound good, but in truth that's just a chaotic fantasy. It's sitting down to play a game without any rules. It's a commitment-phobe dressed up like a free spirit.

I know several people who have made over ten figures in their career—very hard working, diligent people all of them. As I got to know them, I realized something that surprised me. Generally, they have even more commitments, more contracts and more promises than most of us deal with. They know that commitment yields growth.

And that's what this all keeps coming back to: commitment. It's the ultimate antidote to the poisonous seep of self-doubt that is paralyzing your potential and killing your dreams. But before we address exactly how to inject ourselves with a concentrated dose of commitment, let's take a moment to address the question of how to choose your commitments wisely.

Stoic Choices

We're faced with more options than ever these days. Every time I walk into the grocery store, I'm stunned by ketchup options alone: organic, nonorganic, 100 percent natural, 50 percent less sugar, no salt, sweetened with honey, blended with veggies, easy-squeeze, classic size . . . and that's just one brand! Extrapolate that to the options you have for what to do for work, where to invest, who to marry, where to live. . . . We are inundated with options. That's the contradiction of choice, first identified by Barry Schwartz in his book *The Paradox of Choice*, in which he wrote that having too many choices does not lead to more happiness, it leads to less.[5] So how do we know what to commit to?

Never committing is an attractive trap. You might be so aware of options or overwhelmed by options that you never commit. It will leave you with all your precious options, but none of the results. Without committing to certain and specific things, you have infinite potential without any realized results.

Limitless options are a relatively modern-day problem, but we can take our solution from the pages of history. The ancient Stoics used a phrase to help them focus in on their priorities in life: *memento mori*. Translation: "Remember you must die."[6]

One of the things I've learned on this journey is that almost every one of us has some idea of what legacy we'd like for our lives. We may wish to make a difference in our profession, our community or even our family. Remembering the concept of *memento mori* helps us stay focused on the big picture while treating each day as a gift by not wasting time on trivial things.

Bronnie Ware, palliative care worker and author of the international bestseller *The Top Five Regrets of the Dying*, says the number one deathbed regret is "I wish I'd had the courage to live a life true to myself, not the life others expected of me."[7] Unfortunately, this clarity comes when it's too late to do much about it.

The concept of *memento mori* also forces you to confront your mortality. From this vantage point, it becomes much clearer what commitment is worth choosing, instead of waiting for end-of-life regrets. It also reminds you that when you commit, you are committing your most valuable resource—not your latest bitcoins, not your savings—your time. Time is the only investment that makes things truly meaningful. If life were unlimited, you could do all things, even sample all the varieties of ketchup. Because it's finite, it's the most valuable investment you can make, so spend it where it matters.

The flip side to making a commitment—choosing something—is the awareness that you are deciding to *not* do other things. The word *decide* comes from the Latin *cide*, for *kill*, as in, killing your alternatives.[8] Closing the door on a possibility can also be uncomfortable, and you may grieve the loss of that alternative path. But it is also powerful. Better you choose than let the fateful hand of time decide for you.

This is serious stuff. Commitment isn't for the faint of heart, which is why it is at the center of all great success. So, choose the commitments that are at the heart of what matters most to you, and then go all-in. *Memento mori*, time is of the essence, so let's turn now to how to use it most efficiently to blast through self-doubt and rocket your way to the results you want.

Get a Tattoo

There's a lot of bad advice floating around out there suggesting that when it comes to big ambitions, they are best kept to yourself. Better to let your future success speak for you. On the surface, this may seem reasonable, but look a little closer and you can see this is a strategy to cope with self-doubt, a protection mechanism just in case you fail.

President Kennedy did the opposite: he stepped up and declared his lunar commitment before there was any guarantee of success. He went all-in. He Got a Tattoo.

There are many ways to Get a Tattoo—by sharing your goals publicly, investing money, signing legal agreements—what matters is the commitment (and following through, obviously). As uncomfortable as it may be, Getting a Tattoo actually simplifies things. You no longer worry about all the options that came before. It's a guaranteed way to get you unstuck from wherever you might be—in business, relationships, finances or anything else—because it forces you to move. All these ways of Getting a Tattoo are designed to help you keep your word when you encounter the times when it would be easier not to.

Get a Tattoo with Words

The simplest way to Get a Tattoo is with your words. Write or say aloud what you're committed to doing, with enough specificity that it's clear. The best way to do it goes like this:

I WILL finally start my dream business this week!

I WILL run a marathon this fall!

I WILL make that cold call now!

I WILL _____*! (Your specific commitment here.)*

"But, Sterling, how can I promise when I'm not sure I can? I can't commit if I don't know how I'll do it!"

That certainly sounds like a logical excuse, but it's an excuse nonetheless. The point is that you don't know exactly how, and you can't know what will come next, but you do know that you're the kind of person who will figure out what to do when issues arise. Of course, don't commit to things that are truly impossible by the laws of physics and you know you cannot fulfill, but anything else is fair game. When you don't commit, you're adding more uncertainty and confusion into an already very uncertain world.

Herbert Fisher and Zelmyra Fisher hold (as of this writing) the Guinness World Record for the longest marriage, spanning almost eighty-seven years.[9] There's no way they had any idea of the future they'd have, and yet they were able to commit with the words "I do"—just like millions around the world do—and figure it out. It's the same for you.

When you say "I will"—or other committed language like "I do," or "I promise"—it anchors you to the present moment (where all action takes place) and forces you to take stock of what you'll need to fulfill your commitment. Language is powerful. When we speak our intentions, our subconscious mind (remember that RAS) is activated to come on board and help with the challenge.

Putting it in writing is even better. Write it in your journal, send it in an email, put it in a newsletter—it doesn't matter—the written word signals to our mind, perhaps even more strongly than spoken words, that a contract has been made. Speaking of contracts, make it a legally binding contract too, if the situation calls for it. Legal agreements can be your friend because they're spelling out that commitment in even more detail.

It's not easy to go out on a limb and declare something before you know how you're going to do it. But you don't need to be ready in order to Get a Tattoo. All you need is the courage to step away from what you already know, who you already are and the results you already have and instead choose *I WILL*.

Get a Tattoo with Money

Commitment goes beyond just words. It's also about your bank account. I'm not suggesting you pull your retirement account and invest it in a new venture (I'm also not suggesting not to do that), but you can Get a Tattoo with money.

If you liquidate your savings account to start your new business, that's committing with money.

If you hire a company to perform a social media campaign for your new book, that's committing with money.

When you purchase a course to learn how to use new accounting software, that's committing with money.

If you buy plane tickets a year in advance for a Bahamas vacation, that's committing with money, too.

For money commitments to matter, to you personally or to your business, they need to be meaningful relative to how much money you have. If Jeff Bezos commits to a vacation by purchasing a flight way ahead of time, that's not all that much of a commitment. But taking billions of his own dollars to build a rocket to take him to space—now that's a tattoo!

Get a Tattoo with Purpose

Dian Fossey worked tirelessly to document, understand and protect the gorillas of Africa from the powerful global poaching chain that was (and still is) driving this great ape to extinction. She worked through dangerous conditions and political strife, and drained her personal bank account to get the funds she needed when she wasn't able to procure enough from donations. She ultimately gave her life for her vision when she was killed in Rwanda in 1985. But her famous book, *Gorillas in the Mist*, brought the world's attention and action to her lifelong cause, and her legacy is carried on today by thousands who were moved by her work and sacrifice.[10]

I'm not suggesting you have to expose yourself to mortal danger for your vision. Remember, there's a difference between discomfort and danger, but you can Get a Tattoo with purpose. Friedrich Nietzsche, the German philosopher, said, "He who has a why to live for can bear almost any how."[11] The same can be said for commitment. If you know the larger purpose behind your commitment—or your *why*—then this will guide you as you move through figuring out *how*.

Getting a Tattoo with purpose is a heart-centered commitment. It could be grounded in the need for justice—social, political or environmental—or it could be driven by the deep love of someone or something.

Purpose is usually an influencing factor for most of our commitments. These tattoos do not necessarily need to stand alone. Purpose on its own, though, does tend to be more difficult to tap into consistently. I recommend Getting a Tattoo with purpose only when you are committing in other ways as well.

Get a Tattoo with Consequence

In 2016, Denny Marie Post was the CEO of Red Robin, a burger chain with over 550 locations. At that time, she had a serious problem on her hands: customer satisfaction was tanking and sales along with it. She needed a solution and she needed it fast. She brought all her managers together and made a radical promise. If customer satisfaction went up, she'd get a Red Robin burger tattoo. A real ink tattoo. Employees could even vote on the design and placement.

Just like that, Post energized and motivated her leaders, and seemingly overnight her managers doubled their previous rate of improvement. "What had taken them a year to do, they accomplished in the next six months," she says.[12]

Post had discovered the power of Getting a Tattoo with conse-quence—committing when something is at risk. The permanent image of Billy Burger now smiles and waves from Post's left arm.

PS: A tattoo with consequences is effective only if you choose it for yourself. It doesn't work long term if a leader tries to impose this on others.

Get a Tattoo with Your Reputation and Relationships

I've been working on this book you're reading right now, in some shape of form, for at least ten years—pulling together the process, ideas, research and everything else. That work was necessary, but it didn't produce a published book. About eighteen months before this was released, I started talking about it coming. About twelve months before, I told my representation, manager and agents that it would be out June of 2022. That was me Getting a Tattoo with reputation and relationships in order to double down on delivering. I knew that if I didn't deliver, my professional reputation and relationships would be damaged.

You can do something similar, making commitments to those around you—coworkers, clients, friends or family. Leveraging your reputation and relationships brings others into the circle of your com-mitment. Not only are they able to hold you accountable but you have just created a support system of people you can talk with if you need help figuring out a step in your journey. As I wrote earlier, self-doubt thrives in isolation, so this type of tattoo can be a real win-win.

No matter how you Get a Tattoo, the truth is, it isn't easy to do. In fact, it's deeply uncomfortable. Good thing we are becoming experts in hunting down these opportunities disguised as discomfort!

When you are a hunter of self-doubt, you are always on the look-out for where self-doubt is holding you back, and now you can hunt that discomfort to move forward in transformative ways. Denny Post didn't have all the answers when she committed, but she didn't need to because she knew she and her team would figure it out. When you're totally committed and Get a Tattoo, results will follow—always.

The added bonus? Committing to a cause that's bigger than your own discomfort will inspire those around you. Post's commitment moved the managers to breakthrough action. Commitment is the modern-day equivalent of leading your army into battle: lead from the front.

Get Your Tattoo

Pick a goal you have in some area of your life or business. It's best if it's a goal that matters deeply to you and that you've had for some time without much progress.

1. What's the first step you can commit to?
2. How can you Get a Tattoo with words, money, purpose, consequence or reputation and relationships?
3. Use one of those tools to make a commitment now. Get that tattoo!
4. Bonus: Double down on that same goal by getting another tattoo in one of the other categories.

Take It Off the Page with the One-Minute Morning

Every morning, take sixty seconds to identify at least one thing that you will do that day—no matter what. Practice with small things like calling a family member or sending an email. And then start to grow them over time.

This exercise is powerful for building your belief in yourself, however easy it may seem. As Teresa Amabile and Steven Kramer explain in their book *The Progress Principle*, seemingly mundane workday events can make or break employees' inner work lives. But it's forward momentum in meaningful work—progress—that creates the best inner work lives.[13]

You Know It's Working When . . .

The reign of Dwayne "the Rock" Johnson's famous bull tattoo came to an end in 2017.[14] It was an iconic image he got as a kid, and it carried him through his successive (and successful) careers. At a certain point—despite the bull's fame in its own right—Johnson felt he had outgrown this tattoo. But he didn't remove it. Instead, he worked with a friend and tattoo artist to evolve the bull into something bigger, better and more representative of who he now was. He added forward-facing horns representing progress, cracks representing life's hard lessons and an eye representing a powerful spirit.

We change over time, and hopefully so do our commitments. After you Get a Tattoo, you will grow, change course or eventually decide on an even bigger vision—just like Dwayne Johnson—and that's okay! Your tattoo did its job and helped you grow and progress.

When you Get a Tattoo, the belief in yourself and your abilities will grow. You'll actually begin believing you can accomplish greater and greater things. And at the same time, you might notice that life gets simpler, since your focus is now directed on the things you've committed to.

With that kind of growth, don't be surprised if those you've surrounded yourself with have a hard time dealing with your new level of commitment. They might push back or test the bounds of your word. It just means you're doing it right (and you might not have the right people around you, which we'll get to next). Tag me in a picture or description of your tattoo (on Instagram, Facebook, Twitter), and I'll have your back.

Getting a Tattoo might at first be uncomfortable, but I bet you'll find, like many people and businesses I work with, that after a little while it's exciting, joyful and even fun because you're finally working on what you really want to achieve. You're working toward those goals, dreams and ambitions that you've hid or made excuses about for too long.

There's no limit to your dreams. The key is getting started by committing. It's time to unleash that part of you that's ready to move forward. It's time to unleash the potential that's waiting inside you. It's time to Get a Tattoo.

Takeaways

- Getting a Tattoo is a metaphor for fully committing to something where there's no going back, no safety net and no plan B. It's the antidote to self-doubt.

- Dead giveaways that self-doubt is taking over:

  - You think and speak in noncommittal terms.
  - Your thoughts and language focus on your perceived flaws.
  - It's easier to imagine failure than success.
  - You avoid making plans too far in advance.
  - You avoid serious conversations about your commitments.
  - You have many casual relationships without any close ones.
  - You're too picky about conditions under which you'll commit.
  - You equate commitment with losing freedom.

- Committing simplifies life because you move forward from that point instead of constantly being weighed down by potential options.

- Decide what to commit to by considering your own mortality. In the face of finite potential, the best path for you to take becomes clearer.

- Get a Tattoo (commit) with

  - Words
  - Money
  - Purpose
  - Consequence
  - Reputation and relationships

- When you commit to things bigger than your own discomfort, people will be inspired to follow you.

- Getting a Tattoo is a place to start—it will grow and evolve over time with you—and that's okay!

- The way out of self-doubt is through the discomfort of Getting a Tattoo.

CHAPTER 6

Discomfort #3: Exposure

It is still an open question, however, as to what extent exposure really injures a performer.

—Harry Houdini

"STERLING HAWKINS."

At last, Mrs. Danial called my name. It had been a long week filled with presentations on famous figures from history, and I was the very last kid in my fifth-grade class to present. And I was about to go out with a bang!

I'd chosen the famous escape artist Harry Houdini. He was the obvious choice for me given my lifelong fascination for the seemingly impossible. I'd been practicing for weeks. I was going to wear hand-cuffs for my performance and then magically escape from them for the grand finale. It was no accident that I was to go last. I'd spoken to the teacher and reserved this spot. That's how good my presentation was going to be.

I wove my way through my classmates' desks and took my spot at the front of the room. All eyes focused on me. Mrs. Danial pointed a massive old-school camcorder at me, and I saw the red record light click on just as my brain clicked off. Standing with my hands cuffed behind my back in front of the room, I disappeared.

Not physically, of course (though I felt like I was sinking into the floor), but mentally. Every carefully memorized word and prepared flourish fled from my mind, leaving me up there speechless in front of everyone. I was humiliated, overwhelmed and utterly exposed. I'd expected to be the star, praised and admired by my classmates. What had I gotten for all my hard work and risk? I became the laughingstock of the class.

I actually don't remember exactly what happened next. My Houdini presentation was so traumatic for me that I've mentally blocked out most of it. I have some flashes of struggling out of my handcuffs and heading back to my desk to find my notes, but I'm not even sure that I completed the presentation.

I'd never experienced performance anxiety before, and that moment was so devastating that I instantly walled off that area of my life—not going there again! It's too bad I didn't have someone around to help me try again as soon as possible, because the longer these kinds of walls stand unchallenged, the stronger they get. Other than bumbling my way through a few college presentations and work commitments I couldn't escape, it took me decades before I confronted speaking in public again. And you already know how long and difficult a task it was to finally break down those fortress walls of mine around the fear of exposure through public speaking.

We all keep ourselves safe from exposure by building walls of different sorts. And they will keep us safe from discomfort, but at the same time those walls become a prison that will lock us away from the support to develop, the feedback to improve and the ability to grow.

Common Types of Exposure Discomfort

Everywhere you turn there's another place, another venue, another person in which the discomfort of exposure can rear its head. Through my reading, research and work with leaders on their breakthroughs in discomfort—for themselves and their companies—I've identified the most common situations that result in feelings of exposure.

1. Breaking the Status Quo (Asking Why)

Have you ever noticed that the most common answer to the question "Why are things done this way?" is "I don't know"? I hear it constantly, mostly in larger, more established, groups—but it applies to any group. The longer a group has been around, the more likely it is that the connection to the larger purpose has been lost and operations are just running on process. When you start pushing on some of those processes (i.e., the status quo), it can feel as though you're exposed because you're the only one asking. Just ask any consultant brought in by leadership to conduct an organizational review, only to find themselves shut down by that same leadership team the moment they ask questions that might require the leaders to work differently. Upset the status quo and you can expect people to get upset. And yes, you may risk being singled out and exposed as the problem.

2. Doing Something New (or You're Not Good At)

After our early developmental years, we learned the basics of life and likely entered a profession. Anything outside of what we've already learned requires stepping down to the bottom rung of the learning ladder again. This can be especially difficult if you've been successful in other areas. Humbling yourself with, as the Zen Buddhists say, a beginner's mind isn't pleasant for many of us, as it forces us to recognize the vastness of the unknown and challenges the ego.

3. Telling the Truth

It can hurt to hear the truth. It can also hurt to *tell* the truth, as that requires you to expose yourself. Here's the feeling: imagine standing up in a group of peers and sharing the most embarrassing things you've done. Things you've maybe never told anyone, they're seemingly so bad. It feels scary, right? Maybe even life-threatening.

4. Saying No

When I worked in sales, I realized how rarely people say no. Even if they meant no, they would say maybe—"Come back in a few months" or "Let's keep talking." I wasted incalculable time and effort following up with many of those prospects—time that I could have been spending developing leads for actual sales. All because many of us live in cultures that are uncomfortable with no. Saying maybe is easier because it creates the sense that everyone is getting along. Saying no can leave you feeling disliked by another person and therefore exposed.

5. Asking for Help

I'll admit it, in the past I was that cliché male who would rather be lost than ask for directions (or help from Google Maps). When you reach out for help, it can feel as though you're exposing to everyone around you the fact that you don't know what you're doing. This is an especially triggering exposure for those who have been raised on the steady message that your status and value is based on your abilities.

6. Trusting Someone

Trusting someone new with private information or deep feelings, or showing that you care, can trigger feelings of deep exposure. It's like stepping out onto a ledge, as you don't always know if that vulnerability will be reciprocated. Even worse, it might be used against you. You have to know who to safely share it with and, better yet, have the inner strength to not need reciprocation.

The Masks We Hide Behind

Humans are hardwired social animals. We all start out in life with a healthy desire to be noticed by others. All it takes is a few minutes with my young nieces to see that natural "look at me" attention-seeking in action—it's free, exuberant and loaded with self-confidence. As we get older, things begin to change. Many of us still naturally crave attention, but our creeping fear of exposure starts to get in the way. Instead of seeking attention, some of us start to hide from it. More commonly, though, we try to control it—carefully constructing the image of ourselves that we want others to see.

You might recognize at least some of the common masks, or personas, that people tend to hide behind in response to fear of exposure— an idea first propagated by psychologist Carl Jung back in the 1950s.[1] (In Latin, *persona* literally means "character played by actor.") See if you recognize yourself in any of the personas described here.

1. The Blamer

Maybe you know someone who always has a reason for why something wasn't done. Whether it's something, someone or an act of God that is to blame, one thing you can be sure of: they aren't responsible. That's the persona of the Blamer, and they are allergic to accountability. As Dr. Susan Krauss Whitbourne, professor of psychological and brain sciences at the University of Massachusetts Amherst, puts it, "Blame is an excellent defense mechanism. Whether you call it projection, denial, or displacement, blame helps you preserve your sense of self-esteem by avoiding awareness of your own flaws or failings."[2]

A particularly sneaky form of the Blamer is to always be doing something the "right way." I'm guilty of this one. I spent years of my education and career trying to do everything the "right way"—the right way to build a presentation, the right way to dress, the right way to write website copy. If the results weren't there, I always had my defense at hand: "But I did it the 'right way,' so it's not my fault." This had the added bonus of garnering sympathy from others. "Poor Sterling, it's not fair what happened to him. He did it by the book."

But I'll let you in on a secret: what you and everyone else in the world really wants isn't the right approach, it's the right result. An obsession with doing it "the right way" does not guarantee results, it only guarantees you have something to blame.

2. The Cynic

Dr. Lisa Firestone is a clinical psychologist, author and the director of research and education at the Glendon Association, an organization dedicated to enhancing mental health by addressing troubled inter-personal relationships, among other things. She writes that "cynicism is part of a defensive posture we take to protect ourselves. It's typically triggered when we feel hurt by or angry at something, and instead of dealing with those emotions directly, we allow them to fester and skew our outlook."[3]

One surefire way to protect yourself from exposure is to not play the game at all. This looks like sitting on the sidelines at meetings, refusing to contribute to group discussions, not participating in activities and resisting any new ideas. The status quo is the Cynic's best friend because it provides a nice shady place to sit, protected from the glare of any possible exposure.

3. The Bulldozer

The Bulldozer reacts to the discomfort of exposure—and the unpleasant emotions that come with it—by simply pushing through anything that seems uncomfortable and pretending it's not there.

The problem is that emotions aren't like a multiple-choice quiz. You can't just pick the good responses. As Dr. Victoria Lemle Beckner, a clinical psychologist and professor at University of California San Francisco, puts it: "Pain is the flip side of what we value. If you push down your loneliness by staying busy, you can't get in touch with your desire to love and be loved."[4]

If you bulldoze your uncomfortable emotions into the ground, guess what? You're also burying your feel-good emotions, the ones that make life worth living.

If you don't have the happiness you're looking for in life, the smart money is on your Bulldozer persona refusing to feel the things that are less than happy as a defense mechanism against exposure.

4. The Messenger Murderer

Whenever I turn on the news lately (and it's rarely), it's fascinating to watch many of the correspondents who are supposed to be covering a news story end up spending more time discrediting the source than addressing the actual issue.

We all do this to some extent, but the Messenger Murderer persona takes it to the next level. Upon receiving uncomfortable feedback that may trigger feelings of exposure, the Messenger Murderer gets busy dodging the discomfort by discrediting the source: they're not qualified, not experienced, don't know the whole story or just flat-out stupid. The Messenger Murderer doesn't need to take feedback from anyone. But watch for moments when you might be murdering the messenger to avoid what might be true.

5. The Pretender

Being open and vulnerable is gaining in popularity these days. So much so that some people will try to manufacture an image of vulnerability. This is the Pretender persona and one well researched by Brené Brown, who has spent the past two decades studying courage, vulnerability, shame and empathy and is the author of five number one *New York Times* bestsellers on the topics. She writes, "All of this pretending and performing—these coping mechanisms that you've developed to protect yourself from feeling inadequate and getting hurt—has to go. Your armor is preventing you from growing into your gifts."[5]

Instead of being vulnerable, the Pretender is not interested in actually being open to anyone. They are trying to attain the power and connection that can come from being perceived as authentic by others. Notice how this is just another mask though.

6. The Virtue Signaler

Related to the Pretender, the Virtue Signaler demonstrates their good moral values while not necessarily living those good moral values. The idea was first popularized by writer James Bartholomew in an article titled "The Awful Rise of 'Virtue Signalling.'"[6]

There are, of course, good people doing good things in the world. I'm all for hearing about them, by the way. But if you're doing it from a place of proving, condemning or moral grandstanding, it's coming from an inauthentic place. Only you know how the kind of person you are in the world lines up with the one you present.

7. The Escape Artist

I wasn't able to *actually* disappear from my failed Houdini speech in the fifth grade. Thereafter, I quickly learned that although I couldn't evaporate into thin air, I could avoid, divert or escape people and situations that threatened to expose me. It turns out that one of the most popular defenses to the discomfort of exposure is to avoid anything to do with it in the first place.

8. The Addict

Addiction is a very serious issue. Dr. Gabor Maté, addiction expert and author of *The Realm of Hungry Ghosts*, sees addiction not as a decision, a failure of will or even a brain disease: "It's an attempt to escape suffering [extreme discomfort] temporarily."[7] Resorting to drugs, alcohol, sex, work or anything else to lessen pain and discomfort doesn't make it go away, it only masks having to deal with it. Healing from the pain that can spur addiction is possible but may require professional support and conditions not always obtainable for the people who need it.

9. The Under-Talker and the Over-Talker

I've always laughed at the *Seinfeld* episode with the low talker—the character who spoke so softly nobody could make out what she was saying. Along with the low talker, there was the high talker and the close talker— they too were hilarious. These characters always reminded me of the Under-Talker and Over-Talker personas—who are much less comical.

The Over-Talker overshares. It's a "misguided attempt to gain sympathy," writes Amy Morin, a psychotherapist and the author of *13 Things Mentally Strong People Don't Do*.[8] Nothing is off limits for them, so it's common for them to get way too personal and inappropriate, but it's just a distraction from being real. The Under-Talker is the opposite, playing their hand so close to the vest that they don't risk exposure (like the escape artist). Either way, they're defenses for not addressing the discomfort that's really there.

10. The Perfectionist

I've saved the best for last. The most common and maybe best-known persona for avoiding discomfort is identified by Brené Brown in her book *Dare to Lead*. I'm talking about the Perfectionist, of course.

Like Brown, I'm a recovering perfectionist. I wanted everything to look perfect, sound perfect, smell perfect—I wanted everything (especially myself) to *be* perfect! Anything else would leave me either angry or embarrassed. And I couldn't see the dangers of this persona until I witnessed it firsthand in someone else.

One of my early business investments involved a company in which the CEO was a perfectionist. A perfectionist can spot another perfectionist from a mile away. I could count on him being on time and having his ducks in a row, ready for discussion.

What I didn't anticipate was that, as a perfectionist, he always knew the "right" answer, so there wasn't any room for anything or anyone else. The company could not pivot or change unless the idea came from him. Without the ability to share and talk through issues, the story didn't end well—the company eventually went bankrupt. The perfectionist's difficulty in taking feedback was an expensive lesson for me to learn. But I did learn it.

At the end of the day, perfectionists care less about results and more about what things look like, because what others think of them is of the highest concern. (They also expect others to be perfect and are highly critical when they're not.) And even though the world still largely praises perfectionism, it's still just another defense mechanism. One that prevents outside support, coaching or meaningful learning to take hold.

Remember, so long as you are afraid to fail, you will be afraid to try. If you have an environment that breeds perfectionism, you may want to take inspiration from Tata, the Indian conglomerate that created an annual prize for the best failed idea.[9] The stated aim of this activity is to spark innovation and keep the company from avoiding risks. Or consider Nixon McInnes, a social media company based in Brighton, England, that created the Church of Fail. Every month, employees are invited to stand and confess their mistakes and are then wildly applauded for doing so.[10]

No matter the chosen persona, behind all these masks hides the exact same primal need: to be accepted. And because acceptance is so important, the discomfort and fear around it is great.

It's a Matter of Survival

Living a life open to exposure is hard. Again, it is linked to our very biology of wanting to be needed and accepted by a group. Personas are an excellent defense mechanism because if one of our masks isn't accepted, we can always change it. But if we are not accepted for who we truly are, we're in trouble.

In the world of social animals, if a member of a pack is ostracized, writes Kip Williams, a professor of psychological sciences at Purdue, "it is not only a form of social death, it also results in death. The animal is unable to protect itself against predators, cannot garner enough food, etc., and usually dies within a short period of time."[11]

Fear of not being accepted is in our bones. So we resort to lying, hiding and self-deception if it means we won't have to go it alone. Acceptance under false pretenses is, from an evolutionary standpoint, better than not being accepted at all by our pack. But this catches up with us. Our deepest fear is not that we aren't enough but that we will not be loved and accepted for our inadequacies. In other words, we fear opening up and being vulnerable because we think others won't accept us for who we really are. If you are a human—and it's likely you are if you're reading this book—then this fear of not being lovable is one of the deepest and most profound discomforts of your life. But if you spend your life avoiding the discomfort of exposure, you are sentencing yourself to a lifetime of secretly believing you are unacceptable. Your choice.

Speaking of the Pack . . . the Danger of Groupthink

The bystander effect is the psychological phenomenon where individuals are less likely to help a victim when others are present. We've all seen various footage of this phenomenon in progress—a group of passive bystanders witnesses acts of violence against another person when the perpetrator could easily be stopped, but no one steps in. This is because being part of a group diffuses responsibility.[12] It also increases risk of personal exposure. The bystander effect is just another form of groupthink—the classic yes culture where everyone is hiding under the guise of conformity. This avoidance of exposure has resulted in some very damaging situations.

As when Rick Snyder, governor of Michigan, implemented reckless cost-savings measures for the water systems that famously left the town of Flint with lead-tainted water.[13] None in the government who knew of the measures were willing to expose themselves in order to prevent the disaster.

Or when the vehicle manufacturer Volkswagen, led by then CEO Martin Winterkorn, thought it a good idea to install software in all its cars that manipulated vehicle emissions performance.[14] It was a corporate "strategy" to get around the emission standards that protect our communities and the planet. There again, nobody who knew what was going on was willing to exposure themselves as a contrarian.

It seems the fear of exposure is becoming ever more pervasive everywhere we look. The emergence of cancel culture, with its emphasis on punishing and shaming people, effectively eliminates any form of conversation between people and has created an even greater layer of threat to any form of getting something "wrong" in the public arena.

But the simple fact is this: fear of exposure hurts us, hurts others and hurts our world. We must deal with it.

Blind to Self

Kanye West shared that the "greatest pain in my life is that I will never be able to see myself perform live."[15] As self-absorbed as that might seem, he's naming something that every one of us deals with: we cannot truly see ourselves. And we are all dealing with the repercussions of this truth.

Remember we talked about the way our lenses of perception distort the way we see the world? Well, they also distort the way we see ourselves. We have lenses, lies and protection mechanisms in place to protect our fragile ego and identity (yes, we fear exposure so much, we even hide from *ourselves!*).

There are methods around this, though. Every high-performance athlete in the world is surrounded by coaches, peers and others who provide specific and direct feedback so they can get better. Our best possible option to see ourselves clearly is also through the mirror of other people. What are they reflecting back about you? If you're unwilling to be exposed in a way that shows your true self, what gets reflected back to you is meaningless and can offer no guidance for your growth.

The Loneliness Factor

One of the most unappreciated consequences of holding on to the discomfort of exposure is feeling alone. A recent study in social psychiatry and psychiatric epidemiology suggests that loneliness has to do with the quality of one's relationships, as opposed to the number of people in one's life.[16] When you don't expose who you really are, no matter how many people are around, your true self is still left feeling alone.

Trying to connect with someone who protects themselves from exposure is like trying to climb a smooth wall: there's nothing to grab on to. It's your imperfections or perceived inadequacies that creates a handhold or foothold for others to grab on to and create a connection.

You might be willing to sacrifice your tangible results to keep your-self safe from exposure, but you want to ask yourself if sacrificing inti-macy, connection and community is also worth the price.

Go through the Discomfort to Come Back Stronger

Mouse-ear cress is a small flowering plant native to Eurasia and Africa. It's just as susceptible to being exposed and nibbled on by small mam-mals as the next plant, but the mouse-ear has an incredible ability. When nibbled and broken down, it grows back bigger, stronger and faster.[17] With practice, we can become just like the mouse-ear, open to the discomfort of exposure, to break groupthink, take on accountabil-ity, hear feedback and connect with others—and to come back stron-ger and faster, every time.

Let Your Dreams Matter More Than Feeling Exposed

In August of 1963, Dr. Martin Luther King Jr., leader of the civil rights movement, stood on the steps of the Lincoln Memorial in Washington, DC, to address the world. It's a story that you already know. What you might not know is that his advisers, after hearing him practice his "I Have a Dream" speech with smaller audiences, told him that he needed to change it. They felt that talking about his dream was clichéd.[18] He agreed.

King, surrounded by dignitaries and looking out at a crowd of over 250,000 people along the National Mall, started his speech. He stuck to the written script, his voice echoing off the granite buildings. As he was winding up what was a good, albeit mundane speech, something remarkable happened. His friend and famous gospel singer Mahalia Jackson was sitting behind him on stage that day. You can hear her in the recording saying to him, "Tell'em about the dream, Martin."

"Go back to the slums and ghettos of our northern cities, knowing that somehow this situation can and will be changed," King continued, ignoring her.

Jackson repeated, louder, "Tell'em about the dream."

"Let us not wallow in the valley of despair. I say to you today, my friends," King plowed on.

Jackson yelled this time. "Tell'em about the dream!"

King paused. Then he set aside the approved speech and looked out at the crowd before him.

"I have a dream . . ." he began. And changed the course of the world.

We all have dreams. Dreams for our businesses, our communities and our families. If we want to realize those dreams, at some point we are going to have to confront the discomfort of exposure in a way that will leave us open, vulnerable and real. It doesn't always feel good, but it is what makes us better. And it will be the thing that turns your dream into reality.

Takeaways

- Avoiding exposure will keep you feeling safe but limit your potential.

- You may experience the discomfort of exposure when

    □ Breaking the status quo (asking why).
    □ Doing something new (or you're not good at).
    □ Telling the truth.
    □ Asking for help.
    □ Trusting someone.

- It's oftentimes easier to hide behind masks of personalities than let your true self be seen.

- The feelings of exposure are natural—everyone feels them—but without addressing them, they hurt you and those around you.

- You need others to help you move through the discomfort of exposure.

CHAPTER 7

Hunting the Discomfort of Exposure: Build a Street Gang

Find a group of people who challenge and inspire you, spend a lot of time with them, and it will change your life.

—Amy Poehler

IF THERE'S ONE THING THAT PEOPLE avoiding exposure hate, it's accountability. If you're not accountable, you're not as easily exposed. The American Society for Training and Development did a study on accountability and found that you have a 65 percent chance of completing a goal if you commit to someone that you're going to do it. Not bad. Even better, if you have *a specific accountability structure* with that person, you will increase your chance of success by up to 95 percent.[1]

This is why the practice that hunts the discomfort of exposure is based on building a solid foundation of accountability—by Building a Street Gang.

I know, I know—I look like the only gang I've ever been a part of is the Boy Scouts, but hear me out. When I talk about building your own Street Gang, I'm obviously not suggesting that anyone do anything illegal or unlawful here. I'm talking about surrounding yourself with people who are dedicated to your success and committed to your cause, and who will empower you to achieve your goals and grow as a person.

Building a Street Gang of this nature is the antidote to the fear of exposure. This one tool alone will take your results to the next level. Why? Because with every obstacle you face related to your fear of exposure—taking a risk for your business, having that hard conversation, saying yes to an opportunity you may fail at—you will now be accountable to your Street Gang, whose commitment is to help you through each discomfort you face.

You've probably all heard the saying that you become most like the five people you spend the most time with. As such social creatures—yes, even the introverts—we can't help but adopt some of the ways of being, actions, ideas and perspectives of those around us. Right now, are the people you spend the most time with challenging you to be better? Do more? Achieve the things that you've always wanted to do? Or are they validating and indulging all the reasons you have for not taking things to the next level? When you have a Street Gang around you holding you to a higher standard, you'll start to grow into it. Guaranteed.

Your Street Gang Shows You Who You Are

Remember when I wrote about our innate inability to see ourselves? Fear of exposure makes us closed to constructive feedback that can help us grow, but it also makes us blind to our potential, which might be the most devastating consequence of all. We just don't see even the reality of ourselves clearly! Consider this short story from the Jesuit priest Anthony de Mello.[2]

> A man found an eagle's egg and put it in a nest of a barnyard
> hen. The eaglet hatched with the brood of chicks and grew up
> with them. All his life the eagle did what the barnyard chicks

did, thinking he was a barnyard chicken. He scratched the earth for worms and insects. He clucked and cackled. And he would thrash his wings and fly a few feet into the air. Years passed and the eagle grew very old. One day he saw a magnificent bird above him in the cloudless sky. It glided in graceful majesty among the powerful wind currents, with scarcely a beat of its strong golden wings. The old eagle looked up in awe. "Who's that?" he asked. "That's the eagle, the king of the birds," said his neighbor. "He belongs to the sky. We belong to the earth—we're chickens." So the eagle lived and died a chicken, for that's what he thought he was.

A Street Gang will bring accountability and a higher standard into your life. It will also act as your mirror and reflect your true self and true potential back to you. There is nothing like a good Street Gang to help you take flight, you eagle you.

Find Your Street Gang

Your Street Gang can be composed of anyone: your friend, your boss (especially if you have a really great boss), your coworker, your spouse, your Internet pen pal—kidding, not a pen pal—but you get the idea. What's important is the role they play for you. You might pay them to fill that role (more on this below), or you might not. You might want to formalize your agreement with a contract or keep it informal. The right way to do it is the way that enables you to get started ASAP.

Roles of Your Street Gang Members

Any group or organization has specific roles and areas of focus for their members. It's the same with your Street Gang. The following roles may be filled by one person or several people—as long as *someone* is in the role, because there are some serious consequences when there is not.

The Inspirer

When you're missing The Inspirer: Are you feeling somewhat hopeless, maybe even helpless? Do you have the bleak outlook that there's little you can do to dramatically change your situation? Is growth a distant thought while you're solely concerned with getting through the next day?

Without a person lighting up new ideas and connections, and pointing out your potential, it's hard to see much beyond exactly what you're working on. You can get stuck in a rut—not because you lack discipline but because you're not sure what else to do. This is a clear signal that you're missing The Inspirer Street Gang member.

When you've got The Inspirer: This Gang member will help you step out of the day-to-day to see the big picture of where you're going and all the potential within the journey. That new perspective brings the feelings of hope that change is possible, faith that you'll figure it out and optimism that it will go according to plan (especially important when you're committing to goals bigger than you can see how to accomplish right now).

Most importantly, they see the potential in you that you may have a hard time seeing yourself. No matter what storm you may be going through, you can bring your problem to The Inspirer and they will be your lifejacket to help you get through it.

In a recent study on the effects inspiration had on goals, conducted by Marina Milyavskaya and her colleagues at McGill University in

Montreal, it was found that "people who were generally more inspired in their daily lives also tended to set inspired goals, which were then more likely to be successfully attained."[3]

Note that inspiration is not the same as motivation. Motivation focuses on producing a certain result in the short term. Inspiration takes the long view and focuses on the big picture to inspire you to action.

Find The Inspirer

Who is the person (or people) who could bring you innovation, inspiration and ideas, personally or professionally?

The Mentor

When you're missing The Mentor: Even the most astute people need this Gang Member. Without them, you're missing key specialized knowledge in a particular field—the factual, theoretical and practical knowledge—but also the skills and competencies to apply it.

You also might notice that you lack the appropriate connections to the resources that you need—money, time, even knowledge. (Yes, these things do still matter, even if they're not the "reason" you can't accomplish something.)

When you've got The Mentor: This Gang Member offers their time, experience and wisdom, to provide you with a clear, smart and well-considered direction on your path to success. They also bring a strong network of valuable resources and connections to this role. All successful people—all that I know of, anyway—have a mentor. Mark Zuckerberg of Facebook had Steve Jobs. Oprah Winfrey had Maya Angelou. Bill Gates had Warren Buffett. Who will you have?

There are key traits you're looking for in The Mentor before bringing them on board.

- **Experience:** Top of the list is that they need to have experience and some success in your targeted field of growth. If you're Building a Street Gang for your law firm, The Mentor should be a lawyer with a known and winning track record. If you're Building a Street Gang for to your start-up, they should be an entrepreneur (ideally in your industry) who has had a successful exit. If you're Building a Street Gang for your health, they should exemplify the health journey you're looking to go on.

- **Respected in their field:** It could be at a national or international level, or it might just be within a specific community, but whatever the case, The Mentor is proven and recognized for their accomplishments.

- **Connected:** The Mentor is well connected. They've met many talented people along their journey, and if you need to know them, they'll make the connections.

- **Has a mentor themselves:** The Mentor understands the power of this role, and they likely have a mentor themselves. This also assures you that they know how to be a mentor, if you're at that stage already.

Find The Mentor

Who is the person (or people) you look up to, respect and maybe already look to for specialized knowledge feedback?

The Muscle

When you're missing The Muscle: If you're lacking discipline, you may be missing The Muscle. You might have plenty of inspiration and maybe even direction, but you're just spinning your wheels when it comes to moving forward—goals are missed, timelines are blown and meetings are overlooked. Then again, it might not be that overt. You might be missing a person to check in with to report on your progress. I see this most often with early-stage entrepreneurs—there is simply no one they're accountable to, which usually yields unimpressive results.

When you've got The Muscle: This Gang Member brings the accountability, the proactive feedback and the consistency. Let me break it down for you.

- **Accountability:** This is The Muscle's key role in your Street Gang. They will keep you responsible for commitments, performance and actions, and have zero interest in your mood or what you feel like doing. The Muscle might be the first person you share your Tattoo with so that they can help keep you on track. Better yet, if they help you break down your progress into monthly, weekly or even daily accountabilities to get there.

- **Proactive feedback:** We've all been around people who just nod and smile when you ask for feedback. You ask, "How was that presentation?" and they say, "Yeah, good." That's not how The Muscle is going to operate. The Muscle is proactive. Instead of waiting for you to ask, they'll tell you. They might say, "Great presentation." But they're also going to tell you: "Hey, that closing pitch—it was poor. Here's how you can make it better." The Muscle is your tough love, tough talk, no BS Gang Member.

    This also works at a group or community level. My favorite example of this out in the business world comes from Hootsuite. Its leadership realized they had some inefficiencies across the company, so they brought in a form of The Muscle. But they titled the role the "Czar of Bad Systems" and gave this person the task of going department by department, system by system, and dismantling anything that was inefficient, bloated or just flat-out bad. Bringing in The Muscle and tasking him to proactively go after their problems was hugely successful for them.[4]

- **Consistency:** Having The Muscle in your Street Gang only works if you're meeting with this person regularly. Meeting once a year to report your progress isn't going to cut it. This is your accountability partner. You should aim for daily, weekly or monthly meetings. Anything less than that just isn't enough, because by the time you finally meet, you may already be off the rails.

Find The Muscle

Who is the person (or people) who could hold you accountable to what you say you're going to do?

The Heart

When you're missing The Heart: Everyone needs to feel some level of love and acceptance. Unless they're a sociopath. Abraham Maslow, American psychologist, is probably best known for the acknowledgment of these two needs in his hierarchy of needs once basic survival needs are met. If these needs aren't met, it can send us into a tailspin of extreme self-doubt. When you putting yourself out there for your own growth, there are going to be times when the discomfort of exposure becomes acute—perhaps in the form of shame or fear—and you might lose your forward momentum.

When you've got The Heart: The Heart is the member in your Street Gang who will remind you that you're accepted for exactly who you are. The Heart gives you the strength and courage to move forward knowing that there will always be a safe place of absolute acceptance to which you can retreat when feeling raw and vulnerable from exposure. The Heart brings empathy, encouragement and safety to your Street Gang.

Another thing The Heart will help with is recontextualizing your feelings of discomfort. I had several uncles fight in World War II. As a kid I remember hearing my Uncle Walter tell me a story about when he was sent to central Italy to fight on the front line. In the town of Anzio, his unit was surprised by Nazi artillery. Walter was badly hurt in the battle, and he ended up in a military hospital for several months. It was here he learned that doctors treating World War II combat soldiers were noticing a perplexing pattern. They told him that as awful and severe as some of the injuries were, the soldiers generally reported to be in less pain than civilian patients with comparable injuries. The theory they came up with was that the conditions for an active soldier were so brutal, they were just thankful to be off the battlefield. These relative conditions were modifying their brain's experience of their pain.

If you are determined to move through the discomfort of exposure (or any discomfort for that matter), there will be pain. But pain is less painful when we believe we are safe. And maybe the only reason we can get through it. That's why The Heart is such an invaluable member of your Street Gang.

Find The Heart

Who could be the person (or people) who loves and accepts you unconditionally?

Shared Traits of Your Street Gang

Your Street Gang members play various roles, but they should all be sharing and operating with the same traits. It is up to you to clearly articulate these guiding traits for your Street Gang and ensure there is consensus before you begin working together.

- **Honesty:** It's popular to ask for honest feedback, isn't it? It's also easy to forget about it, skip it or let it slide because it doesn't feel good. It's just as easy for the person asked to give feedback to overly soften it to avoid hurt feelings. Real and honest feedback is hard to come by, and one of the greatest treasures from your Street Gang.

- **Integrity:** Integrity is not only being honest, it's also having strong moral principles that you live by. Principles like honoring your word, doing what you say you will do, and not letting yourself or others off the hook. Those core principles should be an important guiding force in your Street Gang.

- **Alignment:** We've all experienced sharing a personal win with someone who is less than pleased for us. They're upset it wasn't them or that you're outdoing them. That may be fine in the world of competition, but not in the world of your Street Gang. Your Street Gang members should all be aligned on the fact that when you win, the entire Gang wins.

- **Trust:** Honesty, integrity and alignment come first, but there are two more traits that are integral to your Street Gang, and they take a bit of time and effort to develop. The first is trust. Truly knowing that you can rely on someone, their character and their intention for your success takes some time to establish, but you want your Street Gang to hold the collective intention to build that kind of trust right from the start.

- **Loyalty:** The second quality that may take time to establish is loyalty. Unless, of course, you already have a long history with that person. Maybe they are a family member.

  On December 6, 1950, *Washington Post* music critic Paul Hume published a review of Margaret Truman's singing performance at Constitution Hall, in Washington, DC. He berated it. She was the daughter of US president Harry Truman. President Truman wasn't just a protective parent, he was part of his daughter's Street Gang. He penned a letter—from the Office of the President—to the critic threatening to fight him on behalf of his daughter.[5] True story.

  Now, there's a lot more to loyalty than raising your fists (or your pen). My point is simply that the president was loyal to his daughter, just like your Street Gang should be loyal to you. That doesn't mean they're not giving you hard feedback behind the scenes, but over time they start to stick up for you, look out for you and are steadfast in their commitment. (Even if your singing is horrible.)

A final word: It is your responsibility as a leader to build, grow and cultivate your Street Gang. Not theirs. You should be driving the meetings, managing the relationships, giving value and supporting your Gang in anything they need to make you better. It's results you want, and you have to be willing to work with your team to get them.

How to Start Your Street Gang

Having a Street Gang isn't optional. Surrounding yourself with the right people will be the key to your success. Just think about it. In nearly every success story, real or fictional, there's a Street Gang. Can you imagine Jesus without the apostles, a president without a cabinet, or Yoda without the Jedis? Of course not. Leaders—whether religious, political, or intergalactic—all know that the team is a necessary component to success.

So, it's time for you to assemble your Street Gang. You don't have to set out to have Warren Buffett as part of your Street Gang right out of the gate; look to the people who are already playing these roles informally. Chances are most of your Street Gang is already in your life in some shape or form. Turn to the lists you made when asked to identify The Inspirer, The Mentor, The Muscle and The Heart in your Street Gang (see pages 104–111).

Put It All Together

Once you know who you would like to approach to be in your Street Gang, take these steps:

1. Invite the person to a conversation—don't spring into a conversation when they're busy or preoccupied with something else.

2. When you find a good time for a conversation, be clear and specific about your goals, aspirations and dreams. It is also helpful to let them know right up front what kind of time commitment you are asking of them—monthly meetings are usually best.

3. Ask if that person is willing to support you in the role(s) you're suggesting.

4. If they're open to it, ask for their formal support. Ask them to be in your Street Gang. Don't make it weird, just tell them Sterling sent you.

The Street Gang role usually isn't reciprocal, though it can be. If you're The Mentor in my Street Gang, in all likelihood I'm not a good person to be The Mentor in yours. But if you have a relationship in which you hold each other accountable, for example, serving those roles for each other might be fine.

Just because it might not go both ways in terms of Street Gang roles does not mean this isn't a mutually beneficial relationship. You should also be providing value to the other person, whether in the form of payment, references, some of your own talent and time, support in realizing their vision in the world or whatever is useful to them. If it's all one-way, it won't last very long.

Your Street Gang can and will change over time. The Gang that you start a company with will probably be vastly different from the Gang you'll need to take that company public. Don't hesitate to change your Gang as you change and progress.

You Know It's Working When . . .

You start reaching your results. Impact, growth and results are key for your Street Gang, not how it looks or how it operates. That's for you to determine. You might find you need more than one person serving as The Muscle. You might find that The Inspirer is found in the writings of a historical figure. You might even realize that you already have The Mentor, you just didn't recognize it. A Street Gang may meet all together, meet with you separately, or even have multiple roles held by the same person. The important thing is that you have the Gang, and you use it to reach the results you're looking to achieve. Actually, odds are that the results will be far beyond anything you're currently looking to achieve.

That was Sabrina Kay's experience when she built her Street Gang. She didn't start out looking for a Gang, she was just trying to stay alive. Sabrina arrived in the United States from Korea at the age of eighteen. She didn't speak a word of English, was a single mother and supported her parents. She worked multiple jobs—as a janitor, as a waitress, in a laundromat, anything to get by—but still her family struggled below the poverty line.

Sabrina was determined. In a recent interview with me, she opened up about her journey in those early days of her life in the United States. "When the student is ready, the teacher will appear," she said, paraphrasing the Buddha. "I had a beginner's mind in a desperate situation. Opportunities are everywhere if you're hypervigilant and paying attention."[6]

She went on to explain how one day while reading a Korean newspaper, she saw an article about how computers would become an important tool in the fashion industry. Sabrina sensed a growth opportunity here, but she wasn't yet sure exactly what it was. She cold-called Lectra, the computer software company she had read about in the paper. When she met with the regional president, John Robinson, she explained to him that she could teach the software to Korean fashion designers and patternmakers so that Lectra could sell more software to the new market.

Robinson decided to partner with her on the training and donated Lectra software to her. "Mentors don't always say they're mentors, but he certainly was," Sabrina recounts. "The software donation from Lectra became the catalyst of my school."

Outrageous, right? But it didn't stop there. She met Bill Clohan, who was the undersecretary of education during the Reagan administration, and he guided her through the regulatory environment to start a college. Her Street Gang was starting to form.

She knew she didn't have the academic or business experience to build a college, so slowly but surely, she built a Street Gang with the support, accountability and expertise she needed.

Her father played the role of The Heart, constantly supporting her next steps and eventually working for her.

Her Inspiration was the priest at her local parish.

And The Muscle, well, Sabrina has a lot of her own accountability to begin with, but it was her mom who took the reins there.

"Even with nothing to offer," says Sabrina, "I still had something to offer in every relationship. I was on time, prepared, dressed properly, listened intently and did what I said I would do—actions speak louder than words." She took the most valuable resource—time—and used it to invest in making these relationships strong. She worked fourteen-hour days, seven days a week, as she started and ran her school, the Art Institute of Hollywood. She sold it for solid eight figures to a publicly traded company and retired as a philanthropist in her thirties. Sabrina says, "Without those around me, I never would have made it a fraction as far."

Takeaways

- Building a metaphorical Street Gang is surrounding yourself with people who have your back and help you grow.

- Building a Street Gang will help you move through the discomfort of exposure.

- Your Street Gang can consist of anyone: family member, colleague or friend.

- The roles of Street Gang members are

  □ The Inspirer: someone to light up ideas, connections and inspiration.

- □ The Mentor: someone to share direction and specialized knowledge in a field.
- □ The Muscle: someone to proactively hold you to account.
- □ The Heart: someone who loves, accepts and empathizes with you, even when others do not.

- These are character traits you're looking for in your Street Gang:

  - □ Honesty
  - □ Integrity
  - □ Alignment
  - □ Trust
  - □ Loyalty

- Those around you help you see yourself and your situations more effectively—your progress is only as good as your Street Gang.

- Your Street Gang members are likely already in your life; you just need to find and identify them.

- To build a Street Gang:

  - □ Invite the person to a conversation—don't spring it on them!
  - □ Be clear about your goals, aspirations and dreams.
  - □ Ask if that person is willing to support you in the role(s) you're suggesting.
  - □ If yes, create some sort of structure to meet (usually monthly is best).

- It is your responsibility to build, grow and cultivate your Street Gang.

- The way out is through the discomfort of exposure by Building a Street Gang.

CHAPTER 8

Discomfort #4: Challenges

*Running away from your problems
is a race you'll never win.*

—Ben Francia

LOCKED IN A COMMERCIAL FREEZER by the bad guys, it looks like it's the end for MacGyver. But not so fast! Cool-headed as can be (and not just because he's in a freezer), he breaks a piece off a metal rack, lines it up *just so* between the light and the door lock. MacGyver grabs some ice, melts it under the light and directs the water down the rack and into the crevices of the lock. Now he waits. But his core temperature is dropping and he's in danger of freezing to death in minutes. Bam! The lock flies open, thanks to the pressure of the expanding water as it refreezes into ice. MacGyver did it again![1]

I lived for these moments. MacGyver was my favorite TV show when I was a kid; Sunday at 9 p.m. could never come soon enough. Week after week, MacGyver would overcome seemingly impossible challenges with his inventive solutions using the everyday objects around him. Did you know chewing gum and a paper clip could stop a runaway train? Me neither! But MacGyver seemed to know everything.

I think I was so obsessed with MacGyver because no matter what problems, obstacles or limits he ran into, he always found a creative way through—so much so that *MacGyvering* became a verb in pop culture.

Now, you're probably not going to find yourself trapped in a commercial freezer. (Although now you know what to do if you are.) But from time to time along the path of doing the work toward our goals, we're faced with challenges that test our abilities. Most of us view challenges as unwelcome detours that complicate our timelines or, worse yet, as roadblocks that prevent us from moving forward. But there's a secret. Remember that chewing gum?

A challenge of any kind is actually a portal out of existing conditions—out of where everything runs a certain way and there are exact tools for the job—and into the commercial freezer where you can see your resources in new, innovative and different ways. Challenges can help us think differently and are an invitation to change our beliefs about what resources we have available to reach our destination.

MacGyver knew this secret. He would even go so far as to seek out challenges, voluntarily putting himself in tough situations because he knew how to leverage those moments to accomplish whatever he was after—catching bad guys, rescuing hostages, saving the day—you know the kind of stuff.

Maybe the results you're after look more like growing your business exponentially, improving your relationships or radically accelerating your health, but the principles are the same. Challenges are opportunities in disguise only if you're willing to engage with them in that way. And you might as well. Problems, limits, challenges and obstacles aren't exactly optional in life. The only people who don't have them are either dead or not born yet. They're simply going to be part of anything and everything, big or small, as you're doing the work you've committed to. So why not let your inner MacGyver use them effectively?

The Bigger the Dream, the Bigger the Challenge, the Bigger the Reward

If you have smaller, simpler goals, chances are that the challenges along the way will also be smaller, more predictable and simpler to handle. There are likely more examples around you as well of how others have solved a similar problem—online, in a course, through your networks and so on.

On the other hand, if you're going after something bigger, more audacious, more transformative, you can count on the challenges also being larger and more unpredictable. You may feel like you are entering new territory without a compass or a clue as to which is the right way to go. Don't worry. If there is no one to show you the path, that doesn't mean you're lost, it means you're a trailblazer. You have the compass of your discomfort to lead the way. If there is a "right way" to handle your challenge, it only means someone else has already done it. And don't forget, the size of the problems you find and solve are proportional to the reward you'll realize.

Globally, we've had a massive challenge delivering critical medical supplies quickly and effectively to remote areas in developing countries where they are needed most. A company called Zipline took on this challenge and developed an automated drone network, the first of its kind. The drones have already made over 150,000 commercial deliveries and 15,000 emergency deliveries.[2] According to investment database Crunchbase, the company has also raised almost half a billion dollars at a huge valuation (total company value),[3] saved countless lives and completely changed the global health supply network. Big challenge, big reward.

Common Ways We Avoid Challenges

Despite the very real and very compelling rewards that can come from challenges, let's get real for a moment. We humans tend to hate problems. We like comfort, ease, knowing the way and smooth sailing. We even pat ourselves on the back when we haven't had any problems in a while! We usually interpret this as a sign of our cleverness or success, rather than the more likely explanation that we're not shooting high enough.

In response to our aversion to challenges, we've developed many sophisticated techniques for not dealing with them. If we want to be the kind of people who leverage our challenges to cut through to the heart of making a difference, we need to be able to spot these responses so we can eradicate them from how we operate. The following are the most common techniques for avoiding challenges.

Dodging Challenges

The easiest way to respond to a problem is by dodging it. This is when you see the challenge and actively choose to delay dealing with it, ignore it or set it aside.

I see this most commonly in interpersonal relationships. Can you relate? You know there is a problem or a challenging conversation that needs to be had—somebody said something offensive, stepped on your toes or hurt your ego in some way—and you decide not to do anything about it. The voice in your head says something along the lines of "I'll say something next time." It says the same thing the next time. And the next.

Sometimes you can dodge certain challenges—like a tough conversation, looking for a new job, starting something new—without them catching up to you and things blowing up in your face. Sometimes. But it will leave you in the same situation you started in. A 2017 study sponsored by Quantum Workplace and Fierce Conversations surveyed 1,344 full-time employees and found that 53 percent of them handle a toxic (a tough, uncomfortable or problematic) situation by dodging it![4] Okay, they said *ignoring*, rather than *dodging*, but it's this same idea. A challenge that is never addressed is never solved.

Avoiding Challenges

Clearly seeing a challenge and dodging it is different from suspecting a challenge lies ahead of you and then avoiding that direction altogether. The fear and worry of a potential obstacle can stop you before you even start. People who avoid challenges typically sound like the classic pessimist in the room—spouting a million possible problems that are going to thwart their goal before it's even had a chance to see the light of day. Yet breakthroughs are often hiding in ridiculous or outrageous ideas.

I had a friend in college whose dad had supposedly created a tripleblade razor design back in the 1980s. I would hear stories about how he was worried he wouldn't have enough time to launch the business, worried about how he'd find buyers, worried about competition. He was so worried he didn't even file a patent. The worry never went away, it just changed to regret when Gillette introduced its triple-blade razor in 1998 and it was too late.

Denying Challenges

If you know there's an inevitable challenge but pretend it won't happen, you're in denial. Challenge denial can work on two levels: not admitting it to others and not admitting it to yourself. If you deny an obvious problem to others, you're a gaslighter. Denying it to yourself is trickier to deal with. According to Wharton School of the University of Pennsylvania organizational psychologist Adam Grant, the longer you practice ignoring facts, repeating your favorite argument, or being stubborn, the stronger this way of being becomes (like any habit). He further argues that we fool ourselves because we feel weak when we're forced to let go of our beliefs. And strong when we keep them. If this is a habit you keep, you'll keep fooling yourself.[5]

Excusing Challenges

The problems we are dealing with as businesses, governments, communities and families are becoming increasingly complex. Or we're just becoming more aware of the complexities that have always been here. Either way, the result is that real facts are harder to gather, the spin complicates the view, and there are more legal, operational and safety details to think about. Instead of opening to a challenge of this nature, it's oftentimes easier to excuse it with the pretense of blaming somebody or something else. Again, the biggest inhibitor of breakthrough growth is the classic excuse.

I've already written a lot about excuses and blaming in the previous chapters. What's different in this scenario is using excuses as the final solution for why we cannot solve a problem. Blaming materials, other people or circumstances is an easy answer for why we have a problem (and it may even be true), but this should be your starting point—your "Now what?" not the end. If you stop here, you'll just keep having this problem.

Having Contempt for Challenges

The world is constantly changing. We know that. But sometimes instead of dealing with new challenges that emerge, people have contempt for them.

I remember how, years ago, a CEO of a medium-size company I used to run workshops for would openly complain about social media to anyone who would listen. It was the classic "I hate social media! It's only corrupting our youth and confusing our business!" Now, those things may be true (or not, they're both just views), but hating them makes no difference. The same goes for having contempt for any new challenge. Actually, it does make a difference, but it's probably a negative thing, because you'll likely spend more time complaining instead of doing something about it.

Whether you dodge, avoid, deny, excuse or have contempt for the challenges you come across, the result will always be the same: not dealing with them only makes them worse. So, hopefully I've convinced you that you need to learn how to turn and face any challenge if you are seeking growth. However, there is a caveat here. If you deal with your problems incorrectly, you may end up generating new problems or making the old ones even worse. So, before you rush out to battle your challenges like the leader that you are, let's take a moment to review some of the tactics you'll want to avoid.

Top Six Mistakes When Addressing a Challenge

1. Not Fully Analyzing the Problem before Responding (aka Reacting)

Challenges are unpleasant, and we are usually keen to solve them as quickly as possible, but when we rush into addressing a challenge, we can end up jumping to conclusions. This often means you don't fully understand the problem, and that may result in a less-than-optimal solution. A popular story illustrates this idea. There are many versions, so I'll present the one I heard at some point when I was a kid:

> *A man comes home to find his dog with his neighbor's beloved pet rabbit, Fluffy, dangling limp from his mouth. Covered in dirt, the rabbit is clearly dead. Horrified, the man panics because he knows the neighbors cherish Fluffy.*
>
> *The man takes the dead, dirty rabbit into his house and gives it a bath and blows its fur dry to perfection, removing any clue that his dog had anything to do with the rabbit's death. The man then sneaks into the neighbor's yard and*

places the perfectly groomed rabbit back in its hutch along with a partially eaten carrot, to suggest the rabbit died from choking on the carrot.

The next morning, the man hears his neighbors screaming and sees them gathered around Fluffy's hutch. Trying to look innocent, he walks over to ask what's happened. Shocked beyond all belief, his neighbor replies that they really don't know. Fluffy had died in his daughter's arms last night from tick bite fever, and they had buried her in the backyard!

The problem the dog owner saw and proceeded to solve wasn't the real problem at all. As straightforward as it seemed, jumping straight in to solving the problem only ended up creating another problem. Just like in the poor Fluffy story, solving a challenge impulsively may lead to a bigger problem.

2. Solving the Consequence of the Challenge, Not the Cause

What we bump into as challenges might not be the challenge itself but rather the consequence of it.

A friend of mine went to the dentist the other day and he told her something she has long known (see "Dodging Challenges," page 120): she's grinding her teeth at night. The dentist offered her the obvious solution of purchasing a night guard.

This approach of offering the surface solution is nearly ubiquitous in every business, start-up and community, so you might be nodding your head in agreement with the solution the dentist offered. But something is missing here, and that something is the key to successfully solving a problem. The night guard might be necessary to stop the damage from the grinding, but why is she grinding her teeth in the first place? Is it stress at work? Improper bedding? Or maybe a poor sleep position?

Whether it's grinding your teeth or the latest headache at work, focusing only on solving symptoms and the consequences of a problem will solve the problem in the short term, but you will also want to figure out what's actually causing the problem so that you can solve it for good.

3. Fixating on One Solution

Believing that there's only one solution to (or view about) a challenge can stop us dead in our tracks.

Ever been stumped by a riddle? Here's one for you: Name three consecutive days of the week without naming the days of the week. Don't Google it yet.

Riddles usually catch those of us who fixate on only one solution. The inflexibility of believing that your way is the best way or the only way limits your potential.

By the way, the answer to the riddle is "yesterday, today and tomorrow."

The way our minds react to riddles mirrors the way in which many of us fixate on only one solution to larger problems. Think of Blockbuster's model of providing home videos by having its customers pick them up in the store. Even as all signs pointed to a shifting market, Blockbuster held on to its one way of doing things. And then Netflix came along and put Blockbuster out of business. Or consider the hotel industry only managing its large properties, until Airbnb showed up with an entirely different solution for travel accommodations and transformed the industry.

Fixating on only one way of solving a challenge locks out potential breakthroughs, with potentially devastating results.

4. Giving Up and Compromising Results

History doesn't remember those who went all-in tackling their challenges but gave up before accomplishing them. You don't hear about early explorers who turned back before reaching new lands, or the big dreams of founders who gave up before seeing success. Failure to solve some challenges is to be expected. Turning back in the face of those failures is for the weak who give up on a real legacy.

5. Giving Up and Freezing

A similar tactic to giving up and turning back is giving up and freezing. If you've been tackling a challenge for a while in the same manner, there is danger of stagnation and going into a type of paralysis that can be crippling—for your results and your morale.

6. Trying to Outlearn the Challenge

Challenges often appear to us as knowledge we're missing—if we only could learn more, we could solve the challenge. To be clear, it's necessary to learn more about the challenge and enhance critical thinking, but I usually see binge-learning about how to handle challenges—in a new market, in a relationship, in a new industry—as a strategy to delay potential failure by delaying getting started.

Think of it like reading a book about how to ride a bike. Learning all day long won't replace the need to eventually get on the bike and then potentially fall off and hurt yourself. There's a balance here. Learning is a vital part of growth but not when it delays you from taking action.

When to Address a Challenge: Finding the Balance between Efficiency and Growth

There is a difference between solving problems as they happen to arise and proactively chasing, you could even say hunting, challenges that may specifically aid your growth.

"Almost all of us end up constructing our businesses and our lives to maximize existing performance and minimize problems," says John Patterson, CEO of Influential U, who has taught thousands how to more effectively work with others.[6] "Survival comes first, improvement comes next." Part of survival means preserving what we've done so far. Unfortunately, too many organizations (and people) tend to overly focus on preservation, thereby sacrificing the potential for new results.

In 1921, Ford Motor Company was on the cutting-edge of innovation. Henry Ford wanted a way to produce his cars more efficiently so they could be more affordable. His invention of the assembly line did just that. Sales of the Model T represented roughly 66 percent of the US car market that year.[7] Big challenge, big reward.

The market changed in response to his invention, other car manufacturers started to use an assembly line and customers got excited about new and different cars. How did Ford, the great leader in innovation respond? By refusing to change. The company was enamored with the Model T and didn't want to mess with it. Apparently, Ford only grudgingly made modifications and finally introduced a closed-body Model T, which most saw as a "reluctant afterthought."[8]

While Ford dragged its heels (or would that be wheels?), General Motors caught up with production and introduced better cars with better financing. GM wasn't burdened with what made it successful in the past, so it was free to create something new. Ford was left with less than 15 percent of the market just a few years later.

Ford's experience is a somber reminder that the willingness to address challenges and find solutions for growth is a lifelong process.

There is no "one and done" solution for your challenges. So you might as well get over resisting the discomfort of problems and learn to enjoy solving them.

The Past Is Not a Good Predictor of Growth

Ford's fiasco reminds me of another common mistake we make when dealing with challenges: our overreliance on past experience. Just because a system, process or cycle worked in the past to overcome challenges doesn't mean it will be successful in the future. To continue to grow, you might need to take on new challenges or approach old challenges in new ways.

Logically, looking to the past makes sense. The beliefs, problem solving and approach that worked in the past have helped you get to this point. But it probably won't be what gets you to the next level.

Challenges Help You Transform Weaknesses into Strengths

UK rap artist and friend of mine Zuby spent years building up his followers on Twitter, using it as a vehicle to put his art and message into the world. The quality of his content, his responsiveness to fans and his commitment to the work of building his image and platform eventually landed him with over a quarter million Twitter followers. That's larger than the population of some countries. And then overnight it was gone. Twitter took issue with one of his tweets and locked his account.

During a conversation I had with him, Zuby explained how this incident triggered a bit of a professional crisis.[9] His Twitter platform had been a main avenue for reaching his fans, and it had been taken away. He was stunned. Twitter Inc. was a large, faceless corporation that owned, interpreted and policed his voice. He had not realized that part of his livelihood and reputation were so vulnerable online. This was a major weakness that had been exposed. But Zuby also shared that he chose not to hide from the potential embarrassment of losing his account or simply allow Twitter to take away access from the fan base he had built. He decided to take his power back.

He worked through Twitter protocols to get his account back, but he also diversified the reach of his voice. He had a much smaller following on YouTube, but he wrote and posted a song inspired by Twitter's treatment of him.

His YouTube fans, along with his now energized Twitter fans, took to Twitter to support him and get the word out to others. When Twitter unlocked his account, thousands upon thousands of new people started to follow him—on both Twitter and YouTube. Zuby managed to transform his weakness into a strength and come out the other side, with even greater results.

We Need Challenges

We are back where we started: we need challenges. Challenges are necessary, and I'd even go so far as to say they can be good. If we were always absolutely comfortable, if we never had any problems, our results—and the world—would never change.

I'm not the first one to put forward this idea; neither was MacGyver. You know the famous saying "Necessity is the mother of invention"? The philosopher Plato said that—twenty-five hundred years ago.[10] So yeah, the concept has been around for a while, and it's been leveraged by the great inventors, artists and leading minds throughout history.

Challenges help us see that there could be a better way. In fact, when approached effectively, challenges can bring out the best of human potential and drive us to overcome what might have seemed impossible—electricity, flight, walking on the Moon, breaking out of a freezer.

Takeaways

- A challenge of any kind isn't just a challenge, it's a portal to potentially transformative results.

- The larger the challenge is that you solve, the greater the reward.

- Challenges are avoided by
  - Dodging—Seeing challenges and delaying, ignoring or setting them aside.
  - Avoiding—Seeing challenges and changing direction altogether.
  - Denying—Pretending challenges aren't there.
  - Excusing—Using challenges as excuses for your results.
  - Contempt—Only complaining about challenges versus doing something about them.

- Top mistakes when addressing challenges:
  - Not fully analyzing the problem before responding.
  - Solving problem consequences, not the cause.
  - Fixating on one solution.
  - Giving up and compromising results.
  - Giving up and freezing.
  - Trying to outlearn challenges.

- The past is not a good predictor of growth potential.

- Challenges, when properly addressed, can be strengths.

CHAPTER 9

Hunting the Discomfort of Challenges: Flip It

The impediment to action advances action. What stands in the way becomes the way.

—Marcus Aurelius

PIETRO FERRERO WAS A PASTRY MAKER from Piedmont, Italy, with a challenge.[1] There wasn't enough chocolate! Following World War II, the global shortage of cocoa was threatening his business.

He could have gone the easy, obvious route: with limited chocolate, make limited amounts of chocolate products. That's what most bakeries and chocolatiers were doing. They were also folding due to bankruptcy at alarming rates. Not that anyone blamed them. There was a shortage of chocolate—an easy and totally acceptable excuse.

We've all dealt with something similar in our lives—a challenge that is legitimately outside our control and prevents us for operating the way we always have. (Hello, COVID-19!) Pietro couldn't wave a magic wand and increase the supply of post–World War II cocoa in Europe any more than we could snap our fingers and make the pandemic magically disappear. But when a challenge such as this comes your way, it doesn't mean it's time to quit, give up on your direction or close your doors. Exactly the opposite. It's time to double down with the antidote to the discomfort of challenges: Flip It—turning the challenges you have into opportunities.

Flip It is the practice for hunting the discomfort of challenges to make them work to your advantage.

Pietro Flipped It. He decided to add something to the chocolate so there was more of it! A little extra sugar, hazelnuts, oil . . . and all of a sudden he had a new product, arguably better than chocolate alone: Nutella. A product that has swept the world, one jar selling, in 2015, every 2.5 seconds. Just think, we would have had a world without Nutella if it weren't for a challenge that got Flipped.

The Ferrero family is now among the richest in all of Italy. Challenges may look like a dead end or a brick wall, but that's just a mistake of perception (welcome back, lenses of limiting beliefs). In the past, maybe you've given up when you've slammed into the brick wall of a seemingly intractable problem. Not anymore. Flipping It will springboard you right over that wall and onto your next results.

There's always somebody who sits at the back of the room when I'm running workshops and raises their hand during this part and says something like, "I'm not inventive, I can't do this kind of problem solving." If that's you, don't worry. Flip It doesn't rely on personality traits; it's simply a skill that you, or anyone else, can learn. Just like you learned how to read, write and do your current job, you can learn the creativity, innovation and lateral thinking needed to turn any challenge into a breakthrough result.

What Types of Problems Are There?

Not all challenges are the same, so it stands to reason that not all require the same solution. You don't use a hammer on every single DIY project, do you? We're going to take a quick look at the four types of challenges, as a take on David Cleden's approach in his book *Managing Project Uncertainty*,[2] and then we'll take a deep dive into the type of challenges that respond best to Flip It, learning exactly how to do just that.

1. Unknown Challenges Requiring Problem Identification

One of our #NoMatterWhat Community members, Nancy Jackson, left a teaching career that she'd had for years in order to answer her inner call to start her own business. She put in her resignation, filed the legal paperwork, put up a website and was in business. And then she hit some challenges. Over the years, she's navigated website problems, payment processing problems, cash flow problems and countless other things that she never could have predicted before stepping into it.

That's just the nature of some problems: they can't be seen clearly before you jump in. These are unknown challenges with unidentified problems.

Nancy was able to navigate those unknown waters with relative ease because she'd taken all the steps she knew to take to prepare for unknown challenges: she Got a Tattoo and committed to her business, built a Street Gang, learned everything she could while still moving forward, and wasn't afraid of problems but saw them as opportunities to test her creativity. If you're committed to a result in an unknown area, take those same steps and jump in, knowing that you can handle any problems that come up.

2. Known Challenges Requiring Known Action

Some of you reading this will be old enough to remember the Y2K problem. This was the potential computer error based on computer systems storing data for four-digit years as only the final two digits, making the turnover to the year 2000 indistinguishable from 1900 and potentially leading to a collapse of the global computer infrastructure. It was a known problem with a known solution. We just had to change how the dates were recorded in the computers—as four digit—but it took a monumental effort to do.

Most of the challenges you'll run into are of this nature. You know what has to be done. You know how to do it. You must overcome stalling, delaying, procrastinating or anything else standing in your way to follow through and do it. We've covered how to do this already: hunt the discomfort of facing reality, Getting a Tattoo and Building a Street Gang. Those steps are indispensable, and you'll use them at every turn.

3. Known Challenges Requiring New Expertise

When I was a teenager, I signed up for Outward Bound—an adventure program geared to young people that offered a variety of wilderness courses all over the world. I chose an eighteen-day mountaineering course. They didn't tell me the pack would weigh as much as I did and that we'd be hiking nearly twenty miles some days. Nor did they tell me that we'd end up in a high mountain basin in the middle of a thunderstorm.

But there I was, facing the life-threatening dangers of active lightening in the Colorado Rockies that I'd never encountered before and had no solution for. Fortunately, we had expert guides with us (you can see how important The Mentor is now), and they showed us how to spread out and crouch down on our sleeping mats with our heads between our knees. Everyone was okay, albeit a little rattled, and sore from spending too much time in the "lightening crouch."

Some of the challenges you'll encounter will be like this. You know what you are facing and can name the problem and are willing to act, but you don't have the information, technique, skill or expertise to handle it effectively. If you've developed a strong Street Gang, that will be where you start. You'll need to gather the information and then act.

4. Known Challenges Requiring Flip It

Restaurants and hotels were among the businesses most impacted by the COVID-19 pandemic. As border controls tightened and social distancing efforts increased in mid-2020, Homeikan, a Japanese chain of traditional inns, was facing dramatically declining business similar to other hotels around the world.

The leadership knew what their challenge was, but the solution was far from obvious. To many in the industry, it seemed like there was no solution. Many other hotels let go of staff, operated in a limited capacity or closed their doors completely. Homeikan Flipped It.

Someone who worked in the hotel noticed that several famous writers in the area were taking advantage of isolation to finish their latest work. So the hotel changed its service model to target those potential clients. It installed rotary phones in each room; trained staff to act like publishing houses interacting with writers, asking about progress and due dates; and created the illusion that guests were taking a step back in time to feel like great authors of the past. Bookings for the hotel sold out within hours.[3]

Flipping It takes the known conditions exactly as they are and reframes, rearranges or restructures them in a new way. It takes problems and turns them into opportunities.

Want to learn how to do it for yourself?

Before You Flip It: Dissect the Challenge

Inventor Charles Kettering once said, "A problem well stated is a problem half-solved."[4] I'm going to walk you through exactly how to properly dissect your challenge so that it is well stated and half solved before you even begin.

1. State the Problem, Not the Symptom

You know this already because we covered it in the previous chapter, but it bears repeating: you must make sure you are addressing the problem and not the symptom when you Flip It.

For example, one of my clients was dealing with poor performance, with team members frequently not meeting deadlines and blowing targeted goals. If this client had just solved for this problem with the traditional greater consequences or team-generated timelines, it is likely they would not have achieved meaningful change. Instead, they delved deeper and asked questions that sought to identify why this was happening, not just how to stop it. They started to notice that people weren't meeting deadlines because they were not properly trained, had too large of a workload and were dealing with frequent company "emergencies." This allowed them to develop targeted solutions that addressed the core reasons for the problem, not just for the symptoms.

Another way to ensure you are identifying the core reasons for a problem is to set up a system that offers incentives to do so. Kaiser Permanente, a health-care provider organization, incentivizes doctors to cure patients, not simply treat them.[5] I'm sure this is one of the reasons the Centers for Medicare and Medicaid Services has rated Kaiser Permanente four and a half stars or higher out of five for the tenth consecutive year, underscoring its clinical excellence and high-quality health-care services.[6]

You too should also take the time necessary to properly assess the challenges you are encountering before moving on to identifying possible solutions. And if you also reward yourself and others for this behavior, you are on your way to identifying your real problems so that you can actually solve them.

2. Dissect the Challenge

Once you know what the challenge is, you'll want to go deeper—get under the skin, so to speak. These questions will help you to do that:

    a. Why is this a challenge?
    b. Why is it important to solve it?
    c. What's the impact on you or your organization?

You might involve others in this conversation to understand several different perspectives and the full scope of what the challenge might be. Working with others to better see reality is a tool we'll come back to again and again.

3. Look to Your Larger Purpose

Focusing on a challenge necessarily narrows your scope of view. Now that you know your challenge intimately, you are going to expand your vision once more in order to seek the solution. Do so by asking:

    a. What is the goal I/we are trying to solve for?
    b. What is the larger vision behind that goal?

The goal might be to raise money for your start-up, but the vision is to have a successful company. The goal might be to have employees meet their deadlines, but the vision is to have a high-performing team. The goal might be to go to the gym, but the vision is to be healthy. When you set your sights on the ultimate destination, you are more open to finding different paths to get there. And that's what Flip It is all about.

Now Flip It

The practice of Flip It is one where you take a well-stated challenge and put it through a series of questions that helps you look at the problem from many different perspectives in order to shake out possible solutions that you may have never considered before.

Flip It takes work—some real mind power—which is why you must not skip the framing steps listed above—state the problem, dissect the challenge, state the impact. Flip It works when you know your challenge inside and out. Now that you do, grab your notebook and pen once more and let's start Flipping your challenge.

We do this through a series of exercises that will start to shift your context and the set of beliefs you have about yourself or the world.

Bear with me here. There actually is no such thing as a challenge (or a breakthrough) until you give a thing context. A car out of gas isn't a challenge for the car, the world or even for you until you're in the context of trying to get to work on time. That said, the problem you're encountering is only a problem because of the context through which you're approaching it.

You can't magically summon more money, more time or more resources to make the challenge go away, but you *can* shift the context of how you see your current resources so they lead in an alternate way to the result you want.

Perspective 1: Do the Opposite

Michael Dubin was at a cocktail party when he learned about a challenge a friend's father-in-law had: a warehouse full of razor blades that needed to be sold.[7] In the early 2000s, men's razor blades was a serious and expensive business. Companies like Gillette and Schick were adding additional blades, bevels and batteries to their products, making it an increasingly expensive proposition for a man to go without a beard. His friend's father-in-law didn't have the capability to develop his own innovations to drive up the price of his razor blades, and selling them to the big companies would have resulted in a significant fiscal loss.

Michael wanted to help. Once fully invested in the cause, both financially and emotionally, Michael thought: What about doing the opposite? Instead of blades that are expensive and full of features, what about an inexpensive, simple blade that would just get the job done? Paired with a Viral Launch video, it was the beginning of what is today Dollar Shave Club, which in 2016 sold to Unilever for a reported 1 billion dollars.[8]

When looking at a problem, consider the opposite of how everyone else is doing it. The opposite may not be your breakthrough result, but it will likely get you thinking in a new direction.

Opposite Outcomes

The questions in this and the following Flip It exercises should be answered with the *same* challenge in mind.

1. How is your problem traditionally solved?
2. What's the opposite of that?
3. Speculate on new ideas that come from looking at the opposite . . . Sure, the opposite of expensive razors is really cheap ones, but what would that look like? How could it be marketed? How would it be communicated?

Perspective 2: Borrow from Someone Else / a Different Field

In World War I, entrenched armies were facing a challenge, namely they were entrenched. Both sides were holed up in trenches and going nowhere fast. Soldiers were getting ill and even dying from sitting around in the horrid and stagnant conditions.

The inspiration for how to break that challenge came from a different branch of the military entirely: the navy. It had boats that were well armed and well armored; why couldn't something similar be created for land?[9] And thus tanks were born. Not only did tanks break the gridlock of fighting in trenches, they've been a major part of most militaries ever since. When stuck on a challenge, consider what other fields you might be able to borrow from to create a breakthrough result.

Borrow Something

1. What other fields have solved a similar challenge?
2. Is there anything you can borrow from them?

Perspective 3: Challenge Assumptions

Ted Ryce is a world-renown fitness trainer of the stars, a podcaster and a good friend of mine. He recounted a story to me about how a training client of his didn't have time to work out at the gym because he had to take care of his son.[10] Ted worked with this client to challenge his assumption that he had to go to the gym to work out. Letting go of the assumption, his client realized that could hit the same heart rate and cardio exercise when he played hard with his son. Challenge defeated. When facing a problem, always remember to challenge your assumptions around it before calling it quits.

Assumption Alteration

1. What conditions around the challenge are you assuming to be true?
2. Which of those assumptions might you change to achieve your desired result?

Perspective 4: Pretend You're Someone Else

Have you ever noticed that it's easier to solve other people's problems than your own? When you listen to a friend or coworker, it often seems immediately clear why they have the problem and how to solve it. (Although, of course, they might not always want your advice.) And if you're able to do that with someone else, why not put that ability to work on your own challenges?

Imagine you are your friend, coworker or even your mentor or idol, and now look at yourself. What do you see? Simply changing who is doing the looking can sometimes shed light on the solution.

Be Someone Else

1. Pick a friend, coworker, mentor or idol (or if you really want to have some fun, a superhero).
2. How would that person solve your challenge?
3. Pick another person from the list and answer the question again.

Perspective 5: Look to Books and Films

We're used to seeing documentaries about incredible breakthroughs—for instance, *The Founder* about McDonald's and *The Social Network* about Facebook, but what if there was an idea in a fictional story, movie or TV show that you could borrow in real life? Sci-fi has predicted countless breakthroughs; it could be there that you find the inspiration for yours.

Look to a Book

1. Can you think of any books, movies or TV shows where a challenge similar to yours is encountered?
2. How is it solved?
3. What can you borrow from that story to support a breakthrough result of your own?

Perspective 6: The Unexpected

Josh Linkner, who I mentioned earlier in the book, is an entrepreneur who has been very successful several times over. Years back, he had a massive deal on the horizon for his software company at the time, ePrize. The potential deal was with the large holding company Conagra, but it kept delaying. Josh ran into the executive responsible for the deal at an industry event and was totally blown off. It was clear the deal wasn't a priority for Conagra, but as the CEO of a fledgling company, that was a big problem for Josh.

Josh ran into the same executive at the airport, and they chatted briefly. He learned they were on the same flight. Frequent-flyer Josh had his ticket upgraded, for the seat next to the executive. It was the perfect chance to pitch him in person.

That's what you'd expect him to do, right? And it may have worked, it may not have. Instead, Josh did the unexpected. He offered his seat to the executive's wife. During their brief chat, Josh had also learned that she was traveling with her husband but in economy class (whether she actually wanted to sit with him was another matter). Josh swapped seats with her.

Upon landing, an email arrived in Josh's inbox announcing that the Conagra deal was signed. The executive had been entertaining a deal with several other companies as well and was trying to decide which of the two was the more innovative and open to doing the unexpected. Josh proved that his company was by doing the unexpected. It was a deal worth 30 million dollars.[11]

We can all do the unexpected from time to time, and that might just solve the challenge we're up against.

From Left Field

1. What does everyone expect you to do when facing a certain problem?
2. What's an unexpected step you can take?
3. What's another one?

Perspective 7: Add or Remove Something

Ben & Jerry's ice cream, loved by millions, was faced with a challenge precisely because it was loved by millions. Whenever the company stopped producing flavors that weren't selling as well as the others, the avid fans of those flavors were not happy. Nobody wants unhappy—and vocal—customers.

Ben & Jerry's created a "flavor graveyard"—a physical graveyard for the dearly "de-pinted" in the company's Vermont backyard.[12] Customers could visit the actual site—or the online version—to pay homage to the flavor and get a kick out of the witty tombstone engraving. They could also request to "resurrect" the flavor. If enough people voted to resurrect it, the flavor went back into circulation.

Adding something new or taking something away might take your challenge in a new direction and open up a new result.

Plus or Minus

1. What might you add to the circumstances creating your challenge?
2. What might you take away from the circumstances creating your challenge?

Perspective 8: Think Even Bigger

It was 1992 and Richard Branson wanted the Virgin Atlantic fleet to be the most modern in entertainment. But it was the middle of a recession, and the company didn't have 10 million pounds to install individual TV screens in all its planes.[13] So Branson thought bigger.

He picked up the phone and called the Boeing CEO, Philip Condit.

He offered to buy ten brand-new 747-400s, but only if Boeing would throw in seat-back video equipment in economy class. Condit, amazed that anyone was buying planes in a recession, agreed. Branson then did the same thing with Airbus. With a few more calls, he realized that it was far easier to raise 4 billion pounds in credit than find 10 million pounds to retrofit his old planes. Not only did he get the latest in media on his new planes but he now had an entirely new fleet (and the cheapest prices he'd ever seen before or since).

Challenges may no longer be challenges when you think bigger than where you started. The natural inclination is to think smaller, dial back and be cautious. There's a lot of competition on that side of the playing field, because most everyone does it. Thinking bigger separates you from the pack and just might be what you need to turn a challenge into a breakthrough.

Bigger to Breakthrough

1. Imagine what would it look like if your goal or vision was even bigger.
2. What new actions or ideas does that open up?

Perspective 9: Add New Constraints

I have one last trick for you, as counterintuitive as it may seem. It's a secret for taking things further, faster. Ready? Add new constraints. Up the ante on your goals, condense the timelines and see where you end up.

GE Healthcare's ECG (electrocardiogram) analysis system was due for an upgrade. GE didn't increase the development budget, or even keep it the same. It cut the budget to about one-twelfth of what it was and limited the upgrading time to eighteen months. On top of that, the machines needed to be portable, scan at a low cost and be battery operated—all new constraints that forced the team working on it to get more innovative, to get more creative and to think differently (thank you, Steve Jobs).

Postmortem research on the project revealed that the development effort was a success not despite those limitations but because of them.[14] GE Healthcare's MAC 400 ECG machine ended up revolutionizing rural access to medical care.

Common wisdom will tell you that challenges are the result of constraints or limits. And that may be true, but eliminating them leads to complacency and a default path of least resistance. The secret to taking things even further might be adding more constraints to achieve breakthrough results.

Constrain Yourself

1. What if you had to solve the challenge twice as fast?
2. What if you had to solve the challenge with half the budget?
3. What if you had to solve the challenge with half the people involved?
4. What new ideas or actions can you see to take?

Using Flip It to Create Opportunities

Now that I've walked you through exactly how to apply Flip It to the challenges you are facing, you can take it one step further and use Flip It as a method to spot opportunities.

The logic is pretty simple. If you, your company or your industry has a challenge, odds are good that others are running into it as well. And if you've Flipped It into a breakthrough using some of the techniques described above, you now have an opportunity to expand outward and share your solution.

That's what Rafael Ilishayev and Yakir Gola did when they were sophomores at Drexel University in Philadelphia.[15] They rented a townhouse together and were always running out of snacks, drinks, laundry soap and other essentials. They didn't have the kind of budget and lifestyle that aligned with doing one huge shopping trip every couple of weeks, armed with a list that inventoried every possible need. They were students! Not to mention that they were still learning how to balance their time between school, work, friends and family. So they ended up taking too many last-minute trips to the convenience store during inconvenient hours and paying inconvenient prices. They realized that this must be a challenge for other Drexel students, indeed, probably all college students and maybe even beyond!

Others may have written off the challenge by saying things like "College students are just figuring out how to manage their life," or "It's not that big of a challenge, welcome to the real world." Rafael and Yakir decided to change the real world. They designed and built an app that allowed students on campus to order snacks and other "emergency" household items which they then delivered to their door. They were right, it *was* a challenge for many students, and their business started to grow.

Within seven years, Gopuff developed over four hundred micro-fulfillment centers, purchased the BevMo! store chain and rolled out to over 650 cities, with over seven thousand employees.

Flipping challenges into breakthrough solutions can open up massive opportunities. By hunting the discomfort of challenges, you're actually looking for problems (not avoiding them), and by Flipping It, you're creating a solution. The rewards for solving problems, for your company, yourself, your community or your family, can be massive.

Own What You Can't Change and You Will Flip It

Truly embodying and applying what you've learned in this chapter will make you unstoppable. How do I know? Because I and countless people and companies I've worked with have Flipped challenges, turning them into breakthrough results. You'll know it's working for you when you successfully reach your goal—or more likely blow through it to something even bigger!

But some challenges just are. Especially personal challenges, where it can sometimes feel like none of the tactics described will work. You feel that you have some unchangeable thing about yourself that makes your true aspiration a seeming impossibility. And that thing stops you from even taking steps toward it.

Maybe you remember the *American Idol* phenom, William Hung. He butchered Ricky Martin's "She Bangs" so badly that it went viral. The negative reviews of his performance were nearly instant.

That's a challenge, is it not? That kind of apparent negative attention would make most anyone want to crawl into a hole, never to be heard from again. The humiliation, embarrassment or rejection would just be too much. I was lucky enough to meet William at my TEDx Talk in the San Diego area. He shared that of course he had some of those feelings, but he did what I recommend we all do when there's something that cannot be changed: he owned it. And in doing so, he Flipped It.

William capitalized on his fame by appearing on talk shows around the world, releasing his own record and even managing to perform live with Ricky Martin! He turned that initially negative experience by grabbing on to it and riding it to future success.

Owning something about you that is unchangeable works, and there are countless other stories out there to prove it: Sylvester Stallone owning the damaged nerves in the lower part of his face that resulted in slurred speech and a curled lip and turning it into the iconic character of Rocky Balboa. Kim Kardashian turning a potentially embarrassing sex tape into a rocket ship of fame. And Dennis Rodman turning his eclectic character into that of one of the most notable basketball players of all time.

If you have a challenge, obstacle, limit, problem or weakness you can't change, own the result, and in doing so, you'll Flip It.

Takeaways

- Flip It is a practice to turn a challenge into a breakthrough result.

- Overcoming the discomfort of challenges isn't immediately obvious, because many problems seem out of our control.

- The creativity, innovation and ideating used in Flip It is a learned skill, not a personality trait.

- There are four types of challenges:
  - Unknown challenges that require identifying the problem.
  - Known challenges that require known action.
  - Known challenges that require new expertise.
  - Known challenges that require Flip It.

- Approach challenges using these four steps:

  - Clearly define the challenge (not the symptom).
  - Articulate why it is a challenge.
  - Step back to the larger vision you have beyond the challenge.
  - Flip It: Turn the challenge into a breakthrough by

    - Doing the opposite.
    - Borrowing from another field.
    - Challenging your assumptions.
    - Pretending you're someone else.
    - Finding ideas in stories, movies or TV.
    - Looking for the unexpected.
    - Adding or removing something.
    - Thinking even bigger.
    - Adding new constraints.

- Once you've Flipped your own challenges, you now have an opportunity to expand outward and offer this solution to others who are facing the same challenge.

- Some things about yourself cannot be changed. Own it to Flip It.

- The way out is through the discomfort of challenges by using Flip It.

CHAPTER 10

Discomfort #5: Uncertainty

There is nothing so stable as change.

—**Bob Dylan**

THE YEAR WAS 2011 and the social media race was in full swing. The newest photo sharing app was about to be launched. It had revolutionary design and the latest technology, mobile capabilities and machine learning. It had 41 million dollars in investment backing by some of the biggest names in venture capital. And that was before the app even launched. Color was going to be big.

What's that you say—you never heard of Color?

Impossible! The cofounders were Bill Nguyen, an entrepreneur who sold his previous company to Apple, and Peter Pham, former CEO of a successful software company. This was an all-star leadership team. But wait, there's more!

Color had top talent in every department—legal, accounting, IT, you name it. It was a company brimming with IP potential, big thinking, focused execution and cutting-edge intuitive UI. Color did everything by the book, and its development and launch was as close to perfect as it gets.

But . . .

After the fanfare around the launch, things got quiet. People weren't using the app. Color rallied and rebranded as a video-sharing app. Still no uptake. Bill Nguyen stepped down as CEO, followed shortly by an announcement that the company would be winding down.[1] All the certainty around what money, talent and strategy were sure to accomplish wasn't so certain after all.

It's hard to understand where they went wrong. There was no internal scandal that eventually came to light, they thought they were following consumer trends, no fatal error was uncovered. Color really did do it "right." That's the point. Even if you do everything right, there is never any guarantee of success. The future is always and inherently impossible to predict.

This is the final discomfort to contend with, and it's a doozy.

I'll say it again: even if you've planned for all the contingencies, continually practiced hunting the discomfort of reality, conquered the discomfort of self-doubt, overcome the discomfort of exposure and learned how to Flip your challenges, this does not protect you from the fact that it might not work out. This, dear readers, is the discomfort of uncertainty.

What Is Uncertainty?

Experts in philosophy, physics, psychology, statistics, sociology, engineering, data science and countless other fields have studied uncertainty and the unknown from just about every perspective imaginable. We don't need to go down that rabbit hole, though. What's important to know is that uncertainty is divided into two types: objective and subjective.

Objective Uncertainty

Being from central New York State, I've been to Saratoga Springs a few times. The city is famous for, among other things, horse races. The Saratoga Race Course opened in 1863 and is considered the oldest major sporting venue in the United States.

I don't typically gamble, but when visiting this historic track, it felt like the natural thing to do. So I would look up in the race book the history of the horses that would be racing that day and consider the conditions of the track, pretending like I knew enough to make informed decisions, and then I placed my bet. The only thing left to do was wait to see if my horse won.

This is how decision making works in a world of objective uncertainty. Objective uncertainty deals with *measurable* information and outcomes. You will either have the results that you want or you won't. It's clear. It's quantifiable. And there's no arguing in retrospect with the facts of what happened. The horses would race, and there would be an objective answer on whether I won or lost my bets.

Given my horse-race-betting acumen, I lost almost every time.

Subjective Uncertainty

As much fun as I had losing my money in Saratoga Springs, there are those who are against gambling of any sort. Some believe it's morally wrong to take part in something that can prey on the vulnerable and become addictive.

This is subjective uncertainty, and it involves an elusive kind of uncertainty that has us asking, "Is this right, moral or just?" These kinds of questions don't have clear and measurable answers, but that doesn't mean they're any less important. It just means they are subjective and will always be open to interpretation.

Subjective uncertainty can be destabilizing because there is not (nor will there ever be) an objective answer. It taps into ethical questions, spiritual inquiries or purpose drivers that don't always have a solid answer. Because you can't "prove" the answers, they keep you questioning whether you are going in the right direction.

Now that we've covered the basics, I'm going to let you in on a secret. *Everything* is subjective uncertainty. At least as far as humans are concerned. Sure, objective uncertainty can provide some answers over time—win or lose—but it can never answer whether you should be playing the game to begin with. Read this paragraph again, it's a powerful idea.

Your social media ads might provide an ROI (return on investment), but is it the best place to acquire customers?

You might have a super-profitable product, but should it be the only one you offer?

You might be in a happy relationship, but is it the right one for you?

I don't have the answers to these questions. Nobody does. We're all stuck with uncertainty, no matter how we categorize it. And we're all stuck with the discomfort of uncertainty until we learn how to hunt it down and go through it.

Uncertainty Is Part of the Natural Order

Uncertainty is not new; it's always been with us. What's new is our thinking that we can control uncertainty in some way, in a fruitless attempt to protect ourselves. Our ancestors lived shoulder to shoulder with uncertainty every moment of their lives. When early humans saw a rustling in the tall grass nearby, they had to decide if it was their next meal that would keep them alive for another day, or something that wanted to make its next meal out of them. Uncertainty wasn't just about discomfort—it was life or death.

We often forget that without technology and higher-order thinking, humans are prey animals. We don't have the teeth of a great white shark, the power of a Burmese python or the speed of a cheetah. Humans are right in the middle of the food chain. That means that in the scale of who-eats-who, we're right between pigs and anchovies.[2] Comforting, right?

Fear of uncertainty is a survival mechanism, and you better believe that our early ancestors knew their vulnerability and erred on the side of keeping themselves alive. We're here, aren't we? That approach left us with this same survival mechanism today, albeit for usually not life-threatening situations like getting to work on time, wondering if we'll have a job tomorrow or worrying about our next presentation. The trouble is, undistinguished, biologically we can't tell the difference between life-threatening uncertainty or the uncertainty around next year's financial predictions. When confronted with the unknown, just like our ancestors, we will, without practice, naturally err on the side of running from this discomfort, even if there's nothing to be afraid of. Researchers refer to this as statistical hypothesis testing, a fancy way of describing how humans use information to decide different possibilities in an uncertain situation.[3] There's no risk in being right. The risk comes from potentially being wrong. And there are two ways you can be wrong: Type I errors and Type II errors.

Type I errors are false positives. Thinking you see a predator in the grass when it's not really there. You're left safe, just incorrect.[4]

Type II errors are false negatives. Thinking you don't see a predator in the grass when one is really there. It's a worst-case scenario in the predator-prey story: you're left incorrect and dead.

Uncertainty Principle

We've traveled back in time to examine the origins of our natural discomfort with uncertainty. Will traveling to the future solve it?

According to a start-up pitch I heard as part of an angel investment group in Southern California—the answer is yes! The eager entrepreneur was presenting his idea for a time machine that would effortlessly whisk you into the future upon the press of a button. You could check winning lottery numbers, stocks, even the future of your business—and return safely to the present, knowing your future was risk-free. All he needed was several million dollars to build the prototype. Unsurprisingly, there weren't any takers. Despite humanity's fascination with creating a risk-free future, that's not how we are going to free ourselves from the discomfort of uncertainty.

It's natural to worry about what might come in the future. Especially if there's a major event on the horizon. It's also natural (and necessary) to limit the unknown, limiting risk. It's foolish and shortsighted to not take into account things that could go wrong when planning. Physiologically, humans aren't built for *everything* to be unknown.

So, our entire culture is significantly built on limiting risk and creating certainty: think weather forecasts, stock predictions, even fortune-tellers. Necessarily so, except maybe for the fortune-tellers. We need some level of prediction skills or we'd spend our time stumbling around lost. The trick is to not overly rely on forecasting, predictions and preparations to the point that we are closed to things not going to plan—or going better than planned!

Besides, predicting the future isn't even possible. In 1927, German theoretical physicist Werner Heisenberg dashed everyone's dreams of being able to predict the future when he published his groundbreaking paper on what he called the uncertainty principle.[5] I'm not going to try to explain it—it's complicated and has to do with the impossibility of measuring both the speed and the position of a microscopic particle—so I'll just summarize his conclusion. Heisenberg proved that future things can never be fully known. Never. Uncertainty is built into the fabric of the world, making it fundamentally impossible to predict the future. A key point that Southern Californian entrepreneur must have missed.

Uncertainty is guaranteed. It's an unavoidable and arguably necessary part of the human experience. But what you do with that uncertainty is another matter.

What's Your Coping Strategy?

Uncertainty, whether emotional, physical or mental, can be profoundly uncomfortable. It has symptoms I know all too well.

Emotionally, you may experience feelings of stress, worry, fear or anxiety.

Physically, you may fidget, sweat or experience tightness in your chest or a racing heart.

Mentally, you may feel like you are staring into an endless abyss. Because you are. That's what uncertainty is after all—it is you reaching the edge of what you know and confronting the vastness of the unknown.

Instead of dealing with the discomfort of uncertainty, we humans have developed numerous coping strategies designed to get rid of discomfort—all of them to our own detriment. What's yours?

Coping Strategy 1: Retreating

"I didn't want it anyway." Have you ever told yourself that? The easiest way to get rid of the discomfort of uncertainty is to retreat and return to certainty. This means you stop going in a new or innovative direction and instead return to business as usual. If you remember, that can be a sign that you're avoiding problems as well.

Years ago, I was a partner at a creative agency in Los Angeles. I got an insider's view on the creative battle that takes place when coming up with new ideas. Whether for a commercial, new website or company rebrand, there was always a battle between blue-sky thinking and hardheaded pragmatism. Not just between team members either— even within my own self. I noticed that whenever we started the creative, blue-sky thinking process, my mind would quickly jump to questions about the feasibility. It was like I had the certainty police in my head shooting down ideas before they were even fully formed. I quickly learned to quiet them, because injecting certainty like that too early left us retreating to used, rehashed ideas and the same old results.

There is a time and a place to retreat to certainty. Too much of the unknown can be overwhelming to our minds and nervous systems. But doing only what you're already comfortable with will only yield results consistent with what you already have.

Coping Strategy 2: Resisting

Abbie Weiss, leadership coach and founder of Unleash Your Message, had a favorite phrase when I used to work with her: "Change causes upset." She meant that whenever something different is introduced to a person or situation, the natural response is some level of distress and resistance to that change. That's because change introduces uncertainty, and uncertainty triggers discomfort. It's a bit of a catch-22—you are pursing change, but you're uncomfortable with change at the exact same time.

We've already looked at the devastating results of resisting change—think of Kodak, Blockbuster, Ford. And how many people do you know who cling to ideas or beliefs that are clearly not working? I'm willing to bet you know a lot, maybe even yourself. As mentioned earlier, holding on to the certainty of the past might make you feel better but will only harm your future.

Coping Strategy 3: Incrementally Improving

Have you ever visited Boston? I went to college there, and if you've ever been, you know this modern city is made up of an interconnected maze of city streets that makes it one of the most confusing cities in the world to navigate. (This is coming from someone who lived there for five years!)

Boston started out as a small town on the Atlantic seaboard where English settlers started to set up shop in the 1600s.[6] (*Shop* in the 1600s meant mostly farms and all the trades that supported them.)

The livestock in the area would follow paths to different feeding pastures. Naturally, the people would follow those paths to their cows. Over time, those paths were formalized and given names. Instead of rethinking, redeveloping and reimagining the layout, Boston's urban developers were for a long time more comfortable leaving the city planning to the cows.

Transformational results rarely arise from moderately improving what you already have. There's a place for incremental improvements, but thinking linearly to fix, adjust and change the status quo only results in a slightly better status quo. Over longer periods, suddenly you're trapped in a maze of inefficiencies, complexities and costs that resembles the streets of Boston.

Coping Strategy 4: Controlling

Monica Geller (played by Courteney Cox) in the hit show *Friends* was known for being a control freak. She was always nagging, decluttering and micromanaging. That attitude made her apartment the place where everyone wanted to hang out, because it was fastidiously clean.

Being a control freak worked for the fictional character of Monica, but it doesn't always work for us. Especially when we're using it as an ill-conceived coping strategy for the unknown. Trying to control everything never works (maybe you've noticed), and it probably leaves you quite stressed.

If you're a control freak to any degree, odds are that even when you want transformative change, you want it to happen in a specific way—a way you can control. This might result in you trying to force people, processes and even outcomes to your advantage. I have bad news. That's not how this works. By all means set a destination, but stepping into the unknown means you might get there on a path that was previously unimaginable. If you're not open to that, you're sentencing yourself to a life of more control and fewer results.

Coping Strategy 5: Deciding Too Quickly

In 2016, I was judging a start-up competition that invited early-stage companies from all sectors to come and present in front of potential investors. There were companies manufacturing medical devices, consumer products, new iPhone apps—all making a play for the grand prize.

I was a panelist, and although I expected the uncertainty of this event to impact the nerves of the presenters, I didn't expect it to do that to one of my fellow panelists. He didn't look overly nervous, but his behavior was odd. Most notably, he jumped to selecting a winner before the competition was even over. And no, his choices weren't based on knowing the presenter personally. I was confused and curious. I had to know what was going on.

I spoke to the panelist, who admitted that he couldn't stand not knowing who would win, so he picked a winner as soon as he saw a decent presentation. Clearly unprofessional and a loss for the presenters who follow, but it was also a loss for him and anyone else who took that approach. Making a decision too early, not because of decisiveness or committed action but solely because it frees you of that feeling of uncertainty, means closing doors on opportunities that may never come again. Now *that's* an uncertainty that's far harder to live with!

Coping Strategy 6: Outlearning

Just as with challenges, outlearning can be a maladaptive strategy for dealing with uncertainty as well. It makes sense. If there's uncertainty, why not just outlearn it? Afterall, there seems to be a limitless and growing amount of information available. In 2018 alone, the world created about 33 zettabytes of data. That's equal to about 660 billion Blu-ray disks of data, 33 million human brains or 330 million of the world's largest hard drives.[7] And it's growing at an exponential rate. There must be some answers in there!

There might be, but learning and data can sometimes just be an illusion of safety and less risk. If you remember from chapter 1, being surrounded by numbers might back up your position, but it doesn't guarantee you'll get the result you want. As a society, we tend to place emphasis on collecting data and not on the more important part of applying what we've learned. Especially if it goes against our preexisting beliefs (which brings back our old friend confirmation bias).

Analysis hurts when it's used as a shield from the discomfort of uncertainty. It never sounds illogical to learn more (so that few can call you on your position), but it may have you avoiding what really makes the difference: acclimating to the discomfort that you cannot know the future. You can't outlearn the unknown, so don't get sucked into the quicksand of paralysis by analysis.

The Unknown Is Where All the Results Are

Wherever you are in life and whatever results you've produced, one thing is for certain: you've learned a lot! You've learned how to walk. You've learned how to talk. You've learned how to read. You're quite functional and capable already as a human being.

All those things are competencies you've developed. Undoubtedly, you've developed many more advanced competencies as well—skiing, managing people, marketing on social media, cooking, writing code— there's a world of different avenues of expertise and you've collected many of them over the course of your life.

You're also probably familiar with the world of things you're not competent in. Me, I don't know Chinese, how to fly a space shuttle or what it means that I'm a Gemini cusp. I'm conscious that I know certain things, and I'm conscious that I don't know certain things. Regardless, both states are based on knowledge. The world of knowledge is relatively predictable, and we can always add to the list of things we know.

But as we established earlier, there's little growth in knowledge alone, an idea I think I first became aware of in a course offered by the personal and professional development company Landmark Worldwide. We must tap into and accept the unknown, the unseen potential in the world and ourselves. Instead of just adding to the things that you know and the things that you don't know, the unknown presents a world of uncertainty where all breakthroughs come from. Otherwise, knowledge becomes a self-reinforcing trap. You can take my word for it, or take the word of twentieth-century philosopher Martin Heidegger, who reasoned it out in his book *The Question Concerning Technology*.[8]

As you now know, if all it took was knowing how to get the result you wanted, you would have done it already. You would have lost the weight, closed the deal, started the company. Simply learning the steps to lose weight—for example, eat less and move more—is rarely enough to make a difference. There's a reason the gym quiets down the first week in February, after all those New Year's resolutions. It's because our unconscious mind is the primary driver of our behavior. Without venturing into that uncertainty, we're left with existing models and approaches. And we already know the results we'll get with those. The limitless abyss of potential beyond our simple conscious mind contains all the results we'd ever dream of. If we're ever going create a breakthrough result, we need the discomfort of uncertainty in the unknown.

Time to Venture into the Unknown

The time on the open ocean must have been exhausting for Leif Eriksson and his crew. Sailing through the northern waters was cold, and the rare glimpse of land that they did see was rocky and inhospitable.

The Vikings had left their home in Greenland and the certainties of their known world in search of the unknown—with no maps, no GPS, no idea what might come next. There aren't many things that can be as uncertain as not knowing what (or who) might be just beyond the horizon.

Eventually, the adventurers arrived at a place that looked hospitable enough—mild climate, fertile conditions and plenty of food supplies—where they set up camp and spent the winter.[9] Historians believe that camp was set up in what today is known as L'Anse aux Meadows, in Newfoundland. The year was 1001, and Leif Eriksson and his countrymen had unknowingly made landmark history as the first Europeans to set foot on North America.

There is little unchartered land left on Earth, but that doesn't mean there isn't plenty of unknown left to discover. Going into the unknown can quite literally open up new worlds of opportunity and real results. It's only from the chaos of the unknown that can we extract breakthrough potential. The only question is, are you brave enough to step into it?

Takeaways

- You can do everything right, but you're still never guaranteed the result you want.

- Uncertainty is inevitably part of all our lives:

  - *Objective uncertainty* deals with measurable information.
  - *Subjective uncertainty* deals with subjective questions like morality, ethics and spirituality.
  - Tip: Everything ends up being subjective.

- Defaulting to incorrect decisions that keep you safe is an evolutionary trait.

- Coping strategies to deal with uncertainty include:

  - Retreating—avoiding the uncertain direction altogether.
  - Resisting—rejecting new situations, ideas or facts.

- Incrementally improving—improving only a little at a time, to stay safe.
- Controlling—attempting to manage all variables.
- Deciding too quickly—eliminating uncertainty by deciding without assessment.
- Outlearning—using knowledge to avoid discomfort.

- All new results exist in the unknown, and necessarily so.

CHAPTER 11

Hunting the Discomfort of Uncertainty: Surrender

We cannot change anything until we accept it.
Condemnation does not liberate, it oppresses.

—Carl Jung

WITH 10,614 FEET OF ELEVATION GAIN and covering 106 miles through three mountain passes of the Colorado Rockies, the Triple Bypass race is appropriately named. It's considered by many to be among the most challenging road bicycle races in the United States. It begins with a near-immediate climb at 6 to 9 percent grades for about 3,000 feet. The downhill break that follows is short-lived before cyclists face having to perform this physical feat two more times.

I signed up for the race with team #NoMatterWhat. None of us were serious cyclists—one of our community members, didn't even have a bicycle before she joined! For four months, we trained in the early mornings and on weekends, racking up thousands of practice miles. And now it was all down to this final push. According to the map, the final 20 miles was downhill, and we were in the home stretch. The map was wrong. Okay, I read it wrong. There was still a 2,000-foot climb through the last pass to conquer.

There comes a time when motivation runs out, strategies fail, the struggle just becomes too much. This was my state as I stared up at the climb ahead in exhausted despair. I had nothing left to give to get me to my goal. And then it hit me. It wasn't about giving more, it was about letting go. It was about surrendering.

I looked up in awe at the mountain ahead of us. I had to surrender my resistance to this moment. I had to surrender the time it was going to take to get to the top of the mountain and accept all the pain that went with it to just keep turning the pedals. Once I released myself into the flow of what was unfolding, the despair lifted and the chatter in my head ceased. All that lay between me and the finish line was my continuing to turn the pedals—no matter what.

What I gained from our team finishing that race (besides sore legs and backside) was beyond anything I could have imagined before I jumped into the uncertainty of signing up for that challenge. I would have never guessed that, up there on that mountain, I'd rediscover the fifth and final practice for hunting discomfort: surrender.

Notice how surrendering is not the same as quitting. Quitting is passive. Surrendering is active, intentional and courageous. Surrendering is letting go of resistance and choosing acceptance and even a profound love for what is—exactly how it is and exactly how it isn't. Most especially yourself. But also for your coworkers, your friends, your family, your bank account, your current challenges—every single thing. Surrendering isn't just acceptance, it's also willingly sacrificing or handing something over. If you want the result of being in a new location, you surrender the time it takes to get there. If you want the result of a grande coffee from Starbucks, you surrender the $2.10 it will cost you to have it.

Whether you're in a bike race with me or facing something else entirely, you never know exactly what will come next. But if you want transformative results, you have to surrender to the discomforts that will be necessary to get there. And you need to surrender control of how you think it should be and open yourself to the acceptance of what is.

When you learn the art of surrendering to discomfort, the outcome might surprise you. The biggest breakthrough of them all, and where all these kinds of breakthroughs lead, is to your true self and all the genuine peace, true presence, authentic comfort and real, sustainable results that go with it.

Surprise twist! Who would have guessed that hunting discomfort would bring comfort beyond anything you've experienced before? But this comfort isn't found in a bank account, a clock or a social media following. Authentic comfort is in anchored inside you—the true you—and no matter what happens, nobody can take it away from you.

Well, everyone in the #NoMatterWhat Community could tell you this, but why not experience it for yourself?

Surrendering Resources

Growth requires sacrifice. Oftentimes, we need to give up large amounts of time, money and effort toward a goal that's never guaranteed. Nearly every entrepreneur I know has invested significant parts of their savings into a dream. Every athlete I've heard of has dedicated countless hours of practice, tryouts and workouts on faith alone that they'll achieve what they want to achieve.

Olympic legend Simone Biles started training in gymnastics a few hours a week as a child. Her adult life revolved around training—strength training, circuit training, endurance training and, of course, gymnastics—usually more than six hours a day.[1] Besides all that training, she needed to make sure she was eating right, resting well and taking care of her basic needs. For years she surrendered her social life, diet preferences, money for gym memberships, coaching and equipment, all before she ever won a single Olympic medal.

Biles's surrender paid off, and she will go down in Olympic history as one of the greatest athletes of all time. But what about the hundreds if not thousands of other gymnasts who are training similar amounts of time, giving up similar amounts of money, with similar amounts of effort, who will never even medal? Or worse, never even make it through the Olympic prequalification to begin with.

Imagine yourself in a similar position—dedicating some of your limited resources to something that's uncertain. How does that feel? If you're like countless clients I've worked with, it doesn't necessarily feel good. It's hard. So hard that many will simply turn away. It's easier to spend that time watching TV, shopping on Amazon, distracting yourself through excessive socializing or continuing on with "business as usual." But dedication of your resources is a prerequisite of success, even if success isn't guaranteed. It gives you the opportunity of success, nothing more and nothing less. It's intentionally taking the short-term loss for the chance at long-term gain.

Right now, I offer you the chance to come to terms with the fact that you can't win an Olympic medal without countless hours of practice, you can't successfully launch a new product without some amount of dedicated effort and you can't expect to live your dream unless you're willing to give up the tangible resources it will take to achieve it.

Surrendering Resistance

Giving up resources for growth is something most of us understand and even expect. Giving up our resistance is a tricker concept to grasp and also produces a greater degree of discomfort.

Most all of us have experienced some kind of extreme discomfort or even trauma in our lives, however broadly you want to define the terms. It could have been potentially life-threatening, or maybe just image threatening but caused coping strategies to fail and left the nervous system overwhelmed.

"If we are unable to fight or flee what is attacking us, we freeze and disconnect or dissociate in a way that the unprocessed fear gets locked in our body," writes clinical psychologist Tara Brach in her article "Soul

Recovery," published in *Psychology Today*.[2] "We become 'stuck' in a biological state of stress, fear and reactivity."

Distressing or disturbing experiences tend to stay stuck in the body as a form of resistance, whether we're conscious of it or not, most notoriously as PTSD, but I'd invite you to consider that it's a sliding scale—as noted by Dr. Julian D. Ford and colleagues in an article published in the *Journal of Psychiatric Practice*—that many of us deal with at some level.[3] Primarily because an untrained human mind naturally responds to emotionally stressing situations by figuring out how to avoid them in the future at all costs. This is another example of how our big brains sometimes get in our own way. We'd all be better off modeling ourselves on the mouse. Yes, you heard me. The timid, little, much-maligned mouse.

When a mouse sees a predator, it either freezes or tears back to its burrow and hides.[4] This makes sense. Can you guess what it does next? Does it hide for hours and hours, eventually sneaking out and racing in the opposite direction?

Nope and nope.

After a period of waiting, the mouse emerges from its place of safety and heads directly back to that same location where it saw the predator.[5] If it doesn't see anything, it will move forward a little bit and reassess. It will do this again and again until it has confirmed that the area is predator-free. The mouse must do this because it cannot survive if it is continually running from discomfort and avoiding the areas of danger—its "safe space" would be increasingly too small to live and forage.

Humans aren't under such immediate survival pressures. We experience situations that are extremely uncomfortable—a meeting goes terribly, a presentation is booed by listeners, a bold business move flops—and we can avoid them by never going to that space again. But over time, the space we have to operate in will also get smaller and smaller.

Breaking through the "stuckness" of avoiding discomfort is the ultimate form of learning to move through resistance. Emotional discomfort may feel like life-and-death stakes, so it's not like you can just talk your way into surrendering to uncertainty. Once again, when I talk about surrender, I am talking about active, intentional and courageous work.

Dr. Edna Foa is a professor of clinical psychology in psychiatry at the University of Pennsylvania and director of the Center for the Treatment and Study of Anxiety. She works with women who are learning how to overcome their PTSD. During their sessions, instead of talking about what happened, Dr. Foa invites the women to relive the experience in their memory, emotions and all, in a process she developed called prolonged exposure therapy. It's incredibly brave work for these women, and it requires a level of acceptance to push past pain and the vulnerability of exposure that few of us could tolerate. But the women who are able to surrender to this process report getting better faster and staying better longer.[6]

Although hopefully you haven't had such distressing events in your life, intentionally accepting discomfort like that is a process many of us could benefit from. The discomfort resistance holding you back might live deep in your subconscious—fear, anger or grief that has become a dark shadow in the unknown of yourself. You're likely no longer aware of exactly why you experience discomfort in situations, you just know that you feel discomfort. (I couldn't tell you about that distressing Houdini speech in fifth grade until I spent a lot of time looking at why public speaking made me so nervous.) Surrendering, therefore, can be massively uncomfortable, as it may force you to experience some level of those uncomfortable feelings again.

You should be very careful when dealing with deep emotional discomfort, especially if it's clinically diagnosed. There are many experts in this field who can help. If it's not properly processed, it can leave you worse than where you started. However, Surrender is the final step between you and the result you want. As the saying goes, the pain (discomfort) will leave once it's finished teaching you.

Balance Discomfort with Surrender

How much discomfort is too much when it comes to Surrender? I like to think of it as a Goldilocks approach: not too much, not too little; it has to be just the right amount (but it's probably more than you think). Massive discomfort doesn't necessarily lead to a massive breakthrough. If you're overly triggered and don't have the right support around you, you're probably not able to be all that effective.

There's an optimal growth zone that balances discomfort with your capacity to deal with it.

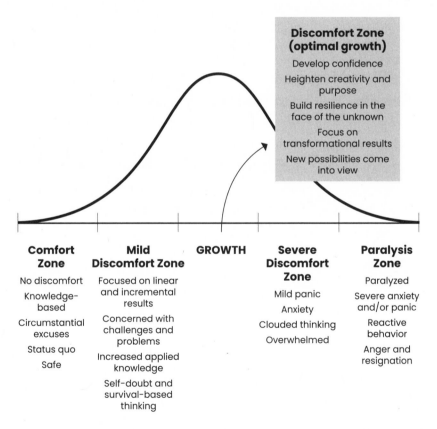

Comfort Zone	Mild Discomfort Zone	GROWTH	Severe Discomfort Zone	Paralysis Zone
No discomfort	Focused on linear and incremental results		Mild panic	Paralyzed
Knowledge-based	Concerned with challenges and problems		Anxiety	Severe anxiety and/or panic
Circumstantial excuses	Increased applied knowledge		Clouded thinking	Reactive behavior
Status quo	Self-doubt and survival-based thinking		Overwhelmed	Anger and resignation
Safe				

Discomfort Zone (optimal growth)
Develop confidence
Heighten creativity and purpose
Build resilience in the face of the unknown
Focus on transformational results
New possibilities come into view

Figure 11.1 The Optimal Discomfort Bell Curve. The optimal state of discomfort for growth.

Let's take a closer look at the different range of comfort and discomfort zones and how they relate to surrender and growth.

Comfort Zone

On the far-left side of the bell curve is comfort. Operating from this place over an extensive period will lead to decline, not growth. If we're avoiding all discomfort and never stretching ourselves, we're frozen into the results that we have. The comfort zone is where we find business as usual, and we already know what that means. The comfort zone is also where we find learning that is exclusively knowledge-based, as well as all those circumstantial excuses. There's little surrender here because there's nothing to surrender to. You need more discomfort!

Mild Discomfort Zone

The smallest shift we can make from our comfort zone is into mild unease. This state is where our more linear results can be found. This is our zone when we're dealing with minor challenges or problems that unexpectedly crop up. Here, we can start to move from theoretical to applied knowledge, but we also have a lot of self-doubt and survival-based thinking in this zone. A little more discomfort is still required.

Severe Discomfort Zone and Paralysis Zone

Swinging over to the far-right side of the curve, the furthest you can get from comfort is not some magical land of growth, it's actually the opposite. The severe discomfort zone (and, at the most extreme, the paralysis zone) are debilitating and counterproductive states of being that produce panic, fear and overwhelm. When we are in this place, we aren't growing and are much more likely to be emotionally high-jacked, engaging in reactive behavior or even resignation from the task at hand. Okay, now let's back it off to the sweet spot.

Optimal Discomfort Zone (aka the Sweet Spot of High Performance)

The key to growth is to stay in this zone, where performance and results are best. The sweet spot of discomfort produces a flow state—the perfect balance between fear and peace, discomfort and comfort, courage and self-doubt. You might also experience fear or anxiety in this state, but you'll notice that when you're in this space, you're so focused on where you're headed and all it takes to get there that not much can bother you.

From my experience, we can expect heightened creativity and purpose while in this zone, and over time, our resilience grows. You'll hear yourself speaking with conviction and using purposeful language like "I will," "We need to for (benefit of the group)" and, of course, "No matter what." (Sound familiar?) This is where real meaningful, transformational and even exponential growth happens.

Over time, expect the sweet spot of your discomfort zone to shift as you get more and more comfortable with more and more discomfort. This means that you can take even bigger steps and achieve even greater results.

Where to Put Your Faith

The principle of uncertainty means that nothing is guaranteed. Sorry. I wish it were another way. After all your hard work, you may end up without the goal you had in mind.

But all is not lost.

We live in a goal-oriented society. You put in all the work to get to your goal, and if you don't achieve it how, when and where you expected to, it's a sign of failure. The self-judgment, humiliation and remorse that comes with it can be too much to bear. At least for some.

I've watched entrepreneurs go all-in on a start-up, and when it's a bust, they collapse—professionally and personally. They give up for some period of time—sometimes forever—mired in self-pity and the situation. I've done it myself. Let failures, both big and small, stop me from taking steps forward because I was too busy feeling awful about them.

So, what's the hopeful part?

When you surrender, any failure or setback simply becomes another step to the destination you're trying to achieve. When you actively and intentionally accept anything that comes up, failure doesn't come with the same emotional baggage to weigh you down. And failure is stripped of its power to stop you in your tracks. You're free to continue the pursuit of whatever goal you have, regardless of what is happening in the moment or what may happen in the future. Surrender is like an emotional contract that you sign with yourself—and the freedom it unlocks within has nothing to do with the events outside of you. And with regular practice, it just gets easier. As you work to accept whatever is arising at each step on your journey, the way forward becomes much clearer and easier to walk.

Would you like even more good news?

Surrendering to uncertainty works both ways. Sure, you might not achieve what you wanted, but that's only one side of the coin. The other side is that you may end up with results that are better than you set out to achieve. You might even wildly surpass your original goals in ways you can't yet imagine.

Let's take, for example, a start-up business that has nearly run out of funding. It's a story as old as start-ups themselves. There are delays getting to market, customers don't sign up as fast as originally planned and market conditions have made the situation more difficult. If you're an entrepreneur, maybe you've been there.

I had a friend who reached this very point during his start-up venture. For the purposes of this story, let's call him Trig. On top of all those conditions listed above, Trig's investors refused to provide any additional capital, and any potential investors were scared away. Hour by hour, day by day, he took the necessary steps to move forward as best he could. Remember, he was surrendering—*not* giving up. With his limited resources, he continued to pursue marketing efforts, continued to call potential investors, continued to support his team. And then it finally happened: the day came when they were completely out of capital.

Trig informed his team, then left to speak at a conference that afternoon, as his last obligation as CEO. He sat near the front, waiting for his turn to be invited to the stage. Naturally, it being a business conference, the person sitting next to him asked, "What do you do?" Trig shared his story.

Turns out, the person sitting next to him was an investor who just happened to be very interested in Trig's company. After that conference, the investor wired funds to keep it going and eventually bought out the entire company, leaving Trig, now the former CEO, and all the employees a happy profit.

You cannot predict the future with 100 percent certainty no matter how hard you try. But as you actively and intentionally surrender, magic can happen in that open space of letting go. Some things never do work out. Other things, though, can work out beyond your wildest dreams. The trick is surrendering to get there.

Hunting the Areas Where You Need to Surrender

Sometimes it can be difficult to clearly identify the areas that could benefit most from Surrender. Again, most of us have constructed businesses, lives and even beliefs to avoid discomfort, so I've put together a list of a few places where you can look. I've also included exercises to help you set clear intentions for Surrender, for maximum benefit to your life.

Lack of Forgiveness

"The truth will set you free," the old saying goes. The truth can also be a path to truly forgive yourself and others. When you're afraid to tell the truth or forgive the truth told by others, it's a critical sign you're not surrendering. Notice it.

About a decade ago, I was flying from Atlanta home to Los Angeles and the woman sitting next to me wouldn't stop talking. Have you ever been there? Eventually, I started to listen, engage and proceed to have one of the greatest conversations I've ever had on an airplane. She even dropped me off at my apartment after we landed!

My seatmate was famed acting coach and now good friend of mine Margie Haber, who's trained all sorts of actors, from Brad Pitt to Halle Berry. One of the central concepts Margie teaches is forgiveness. "We're so hard on ourselves, and habits are tough to break," Margie told me. "The only way to forgive is outing yourself [to yourself or someone else], to let go of judgment and tell the truth."

Everyone has been through difficult things. Everyone. A loved one dying. A childhood trauma. A failure in school, business or a relationship. This human condition seems to have difficulty built into it. You can keep it all bottled up while you blame yourself, others or the world, or you can choose to let go and forgive. It may sound difficult but it's easier than most of us think. Because forgiveness is not a feeling, it's an intentional choice. That's it.

As you forgive yourself and others for things that have happened in the past, you'll stop dragging past hurts with you into the future. Your future becomes a place bright with unwritten possibility.

Finding Forgiveness

Find a quiet place to work through these questions without interruption.

1. Identify one area in your life where you might be holding on to resentment, anger or unforgivingness. (Hint: It's usually in an area of your life that's not working as well as you'd like.)
2. Write out the story of what happened in enough detail that it's clear.
3. List some of the personal consequences you faced as a result of holding on to that resentment, anger or grudge. Have they spilled over into other areas of your life?
4. Seeing the cost, can you let go and forgive?

Lack of Inspiration

The other day I was playing with my young nieces, my favorite little people in the world. They decided they wanted to draw. I thought they'd make a few drawings and move on, but those little creative machines just kept producing page after page of multicolor inspiration. (A few of which are now on my fridge.) They weren't producing these pages for any reward—money, praise, experience—they were just drawing for the sheer joy of it.

How many adults do you know who operate this way? By the time we mature, we have made the transition from doing for the sheer pleasure of it to operating primarily by extrinsic motivation—be it money, climbing the ladder of success or simply survival. I do agree that working for motivation—negative or positive—does work, but it doesn't work well (or for all that long). It gives you a view that's based on survival and getting by, and your results will reflect that.

Are you getting out of bed in the morning because you have to (motivation), or because you want to (inspiration)? Are you doing your daily work because you have to, or because you want to?

Nobody is inspired all the time. But if you consistently don't feel inspired, it might be a warning sign that you're not surrendering to the love, passion and freedom beyond your rational everyday thoughts. True inspiration calls you forward into your full and unfettered potential, whether that be in a relationship, a business or even a simple drawing—and that inspiration can arise only when we let go and surrender.

Get Inspired

1. When was the last time you were moved or inspired?
2. Where were you, who were you with, what were you doing?
3. What was it about the situation that was so inspiring to you?
4. How can you connect with that inspiration daily?

Lack of Resources

Does it ever feel like you're doing it all yourself? That you just can't do enough, don't have enough, can never get there? It may be true (don't forget to utilize your Street Gang). Sometimes, though, it can be a sign that you're overly controlling how something might get done. In other words, not surrendering.

Let's look at the reality here. You already accept help from thousands of people that give you easy access to running water, electricity and, of course, the Internet—at least for those of us fortunate enough to live in the developed world. And if you're not actively involved in supporting that infrastructure, you're probably not overly concerned with controlling the minutia of how it all works. If you're overly obsessed with not having enough, my money is on your unacceptance of things exactly as they are and exactly as they're not.

Lack vs. Gratitude

1. In what area is your progress stifled by a lack of resources?
2. Instead of focusing on what you don't have, what do you have that you can be grateful for?

Lack of Stillness

It's a busy world out there, isn't it? The alarms, phone notifications, emails, family drama, endless meetings and everything else happening. It's easy to ping-pong from one distraction to another, and that's something to notice.

If you have trouble sitting by yourself without grabbing for a distraction (usually your phone), consider that there could be some underlying discomfort in you that you haven't faced. Distractions are infamous for taking us away from the pain, discomfort or worry we have, leaving it unaddressed. Surrendering is about allowing the discomfort that arises when we stop running.

The question is: How do you go into the discomfort instead of going around it or avoiding it? Here's a list of practices that have a proven track record in helping in this area.

- **Meditation:** Any type will work. I'm a fan of Michael Brown's Presence Process. Start with just a few quiet minutes and build up to 15 to 20 minutes or more a day.

- **Prayer:** Formal or informal, whether you believe in something greater or not. I've always liked this saying I heard from a priest years back: prayer isn't to influence the divine, it's to influence the pray-er.

- **Music:** Probably not the latest house music. Choose something peaceful that speaks to you and the discomfort you suspect lies underneath.

- **Nature:** Go for a walk in your neighborhood or local park, hike in the woods or just sit outside. Spending time in nature can do wonders for bringing the discomfort that's gnawing at you to the surface, in order to move through it.

- **Exercise:** Cycling, yoga, weights, anything will do—the important thing here is that you move your body!

- **Be in water:** Take a shower, try a float tank or go for a swim. Being in water helps ease your discomfort, and you might find it makes it easier to surrender to what's there.

- **Color or aroma therapy:** Stimulating our senses in new ways can help us find and surrender to discomfort.

Bonus: For the Adventurous

This part isn't for everyone, but it was very helpful for me. I spent nearly two weeks with the Shipibo, an Indigenous group living in the Amazon of northeast Peru, at the Temple of the Way of Light. No Internet, no power and barely any running water—talk about getting off the grid. I sought out the temple and the Shipibo because their healers have spent generations working with plants. It is part of a rite of passage for many in their culture to go off into the jungle alone—for months and sometimes years at a time—to focus only on studying certain plants.

They become experts in these plants and establish a deep respect and connection that includes an ability to communicate with the spirit of the plant. It may be hard to understand from our Western perspective, but after experiencing some time with them, I've developed a deep respect for the fact that they are working on a whole different level.

The key to their process is plant medicines—hallucinogenic tools that are illegal in much of the United States and other nations around the world. They're nothing to mess around with and belong in the hands of experts. And in the hands of experts, they can work wonders, dislodging discomfort from the past that has been locked away for years. If you go in this direction, be aware of what you're getting into and make sure to do it safely and responsibly. It can be a life changer, but it also can cause harm if used improperly.

Ditch the Distractions

Minutes, hours, days, weeks, months and years can pass in the blink of an eye. If you never stop to pay attention, before you know it, you'll be looking back on your life wondering how it all went so quickly (maybe you're doing that already).

A valuable tool I've found to slow down and surrender is journaling. (*The Five-Minute Journal* is my favorite off-the-shelf journal.) Take time every day to notice every day. Here are important questions to ask yourself when you journal:

1. What am I grateful for?
2. What great things have happened recently?
3. Where did I experience discomfort (and why)?
4. How can I surrender to that discomfort?
5. What am I committed to doing differently in the future? (Write: *I WILL . . .*)

Give Grace to Let Others Learn to Surrender

It's not an easy step to Surrender. However, it might be the most important of all the steps to hunting discomfort because it requires emotional, mental and physical acceptance of what is—no matter how much we might wish it was another way.

When we begin to practice surrendering in our own lives, it opens the doorway to something: allowing grace for others to discover the practice of Surrender for themselves.

This means you surrender how you think other people should be, what they should do, how they should act, to let them go through their own discomfort and make their own mistakes and discoveries. I'm not suggesting that you don't support and maybe even advise those in need, but sometimes the best support you can give is allowing someone the space to figure it out for themselves. It is far better to support someone's journey through discomfort than to try to help them avoid it. Besides, if you step in to help all the time, aren't you effectively diminishing their discomfort? Ergo, diminishing their potential for real growth?

This is probably best illustrated in overprotective parents. Parents have decades of experience more than their kids, and they've learned many lessons in that time. They want nothing more than to protect their kids from needless discomfort. But children must go through some discomforts as part of growing up. And remember, real growth must include some experiential learning—kids, your employees or anyone else in your circle cannot learn from secondhand knowledge alone.

Part of Surrender is learning to take all our mistakes a lot less seriously. Most of us want to live in a good world. A world where people are allowed to make small mistakes, acknowledge them as mistakes and be allowed the grace to move on from them. Mistakes are part of all our lives. If you're anything like me, over time you've made a lot. We all deserve the opportunity to step courageously into the unknown to try something new. And we deserve the freedom to mess up without it being seen as a colossal story of failure or personal shortcoming. That way, we can just take a step back and try another direction to grow in.

The world would be better for it.

Where Can You Step Back?

Think of a situation that a spouse, friend, coworker or colleague is in where you can see a clear way in which they could be doing better. Describe the situation in writing.

1. Write out what would be the "best practices" you would apply in this situation.
2. Are you heeding your own advice?
3. Rather than sharing your advice with this person, how could you support them to learn on their own? (In other words, how can you surrender your attempts to control their life and journey?)

Savasana of Life

When getting into the California lifestyle of yoga, I went so far as to become a certified yoga teacher (alongside about 30 percent of the state's occupants).

In yoga, there's something called Savasana—a period after the more physically demanding poses where you just lay supine on the mat. It's a chance for the body to shift away from responses elicited by the sympathetic nervous system (which prepares the body for fight, flight or freeze, that is activated during exercise) to those elicited by the parasympathetic nervous system (which restores the body to a calm and composed state). Many yogis will tell you it's the single most important part of the practice because it allows you (and your body) to assimilate everything you've just done.

The same exact practice is required when working to accept discomfort. To deny your discomfort is ultimately to deny part of yourself. And accepting it is your path to your full potential and real freedom.

Everyone knows you can't pry open a flower bud. You can't dig up your crops every day to check the roots and then expect them to grow. Sometimes, we need to sit back and let go. Let go to face the discomfort coming our way and let it move through us. You never can predict what's on the other side.

Letting go of your views, identity, judgments is a never-ending practice. But it will set you free.

The way out is through—through surrendering.

Surrender to the discomfort of facing reality and the pain of taking off that life-limiting lens in return for the limitlessness of what's possible.

Surrender to the discomfort of committing even if you don't have it all worked out.

Surrender to the discomfort of facing exposure and the fear of accountability and transparency so you have the support you need to transform.

Surrender to the discomfort of challenges and open yourself to the possibility of using your weaknesses as strengths.

And finally, surrender to the discomfort of uncertainty so you can let go of the past to face a future where anything just might be possible.

Surrender no matter what.

Takeaways

- Surrender (not giving up) is the final step in the system and the antidote to the unknown:

  - Actively surrendering your limited resources to an inherently uncertain future.
  - Actively surrendering resistance by accepting what is and what is not.

- Not surrendering to some level of risk will keep you stuck.

- Embracing discomfort will help you accept things exactly as they are.

- Find the sweet spot of discomfort between your comfort zone (where there is no growth) and extreme discomfort (where there is paralysis).

- Even if you fail in achieving your result, surrendering allows you freedom from the weight of failure so that you can keep going.

- Give grace to let others surrender—telling them will not help them grow.

- Surrendering can open up results beyond anything you may have otherwise imagined.

- Notice you're not surrendering when you

  - Lack forgiveness.
  - Lack inspiration.
  - Lack resources.
  - Lack stillness.

- Surrender each step of the way to

  - The discomfort of facing reality.
  - The discomfort of self-doubt.
  - The discomfort of exposure.
  - The discomfort of challenges.
  - The discomfort of the unknown.
  - Surrender no matter what.

- The way out through the discomfort of uncertainty is Surrender.

CHAPTER 12

The #NoMatterWhat System for Hunting Discomfort

It's not the mountain we conquer but ourselves.

—Sir Edmund Hillary, after the first successful ascent of Mount Everest in 1953

THE WORLD DOESN'T OPERATE IN A VACUUM and neither do the five practices for hunting discomfort that you've just read about. The five components: Expand Your Reality, Get a Tattoo, Build a Street Gang, Flip It and Surrender are not mutually exclusive. They work together holistically and quite naturally—as you may have already started to discover for yourself.

Who are the best people to help you see a more expansive reality? Your Street Gang, of course.

Too worried to commit to your dreams in a public form and Get a big Tattoo? Surrender to as big as you can go right now.

When you do Get a Tattoo, you're naturally going to want to find a way through obstacles that come up and you'll find the Flip It components are right there waiting to guide you.

It's an integrated system where each discomfort is a checkpoint on your path, guiding you to the results that you're looking for. The best discomfort to start hunting is entirely up to you. Find a foothold and start climbing. The most important step is the first one.

Figure 12.1 #NoMatterWhat System of Growth. An integrated system for moving through discomfort and toward results.

A Mountain with No Top

Mount Everest is a climb that's one of the great feats in our world. And yet, once you reach the peak, you've reached it. Our growth as humans is decidedly different. Before being the first to summit Everest in May of 1953, Sir Edmund Hillary had addressed the mighty mountain after a failed attempt the year earlier, saying, "I will come again and conquer you because as a mountain you can't grow. . . . But as a human, I can."[1]

Whether we're climbing a mountain, founding a company or starting a family, Sir Hillary had it right. Ultimately, we are conquering ourselves on our journey of life as we discover unknown potential, traverse treacherous low places and scale the heights to new and ever more expansive vistas.

The mountains of discomfort that we summit have no top. It's a never-ending climb that offers us the opportunity to keep putting one foot in front of the other, using the Hunting Discomfort system of growth—in large and small ways—over and over again. Innovation, transformation, significant positive gain . . . they're not something that you do, they're a result of your continual climb when you make hunting discomfort a way of life. A climb I'm forever on myself.

If you're going through these practices, it will yield success no matter what. It may not always be immediate, but the results will inevitably come.

I said it before and I'll say it again: you don't have to be built for hunting discomfort. Never was a baby born that the doctor held up, announcing: "We have a discomfort hunter in this one." We all enter the world with a clean slate upon which we create our businesses, impact our communities and write our lives. Hunting discomfort is a skill we can develop. You can make the choice to go beyond your current situation, conditions or circumstances and into a life that can be extraordinary. As Sir Hillary famously once said, "People do not decide to become extraordinary. They decide to accomplish extraordinary things."

The Hero's Journey

The process for transformation by moving through discomfort is as old as time. It's the traditional story of the hero's journey that has been told in mythology and religion and through archetypes around the world. Joseph Campbell identified it when he mapped out the structure of the hero's journey in his book *The Hero with a Thousand Faces*, published in 1949.

As Campbell observes, the hero always and inevitably ventures from the known world into the dark underbelly of the unknown. Once they pass beyond the threshold of the known, they meet helpers and mentors who help them win decisive victories over seemingly unsurmountable forces. They experience a profound transformation and return home with gifts to share with others.[2] Sound familiar? It should. It's famously been inspiration for everything from *Star Wars* to the Harry Potter series, but it is not just a structure for telling a good story. It's a set of instructions for living a good and meaningful life—a life that looks a lot like hunting discomfort.

My speaking experience in Singapore taught me firsthand that a trip to the unknown was necessary for breakthrough results. And looking deeper, I realized that the hero's journey plays out over and over again in the lives of changemakers throughout history, whether they be explorers, innovators, visionaries or healers.

We don't need supernatural powers or impossible feats as we write our own hero's journey. You're holding your handbook for how. This isn't a fad or flash marketing. It is simply five tried-and-true practices for you to follow on your own hero's journey. You only need to be willing to depart for the unknown—and there you will find gifts beyond your imaginings. You'll see results that were invisible or seemingly impossible from where you sit today. If you practice these steps consistently, I'm willing to bet that, over time, you'll look back on your life and see it as nothing short of heroic.

It Works for a Restaurant during the Pandemic . . .

The year 2020 ushered a pandemic into the world that fundamentally shifted our collective life. I have countless friends who have lost jobs, lost their homes, even lost family members. I don't know if anyone was fully prepared for a pandemic—I certainly wasn't—but there are those who used the discomfort of it to create a breakthrough.

Eric Rivera lives in Seattle and found himself in one of the worse industries to be in during a pandemic: restaurants. He is the owner of a local favorite called Addo. Addo is known for sending irresistible smells down the street, for beautiful food meticulously arranged on the plate and for Eric coming out of the kitchen to personally greet guests. But it was all shut down in March 2020. The pandemic lockdown forced Eric to close his doors just like every other restaurant.

He could have just hung a Closed sign on the door, let go of his staff and hunkered down at home, hoping for a speedy vaccine while collecting government assistance. None of that would have been wrong, and the emergency grants undoubtedly saved much of the sector. Whatever the case may be, one thing is for certain: Eric chose to do something else as well.[3]

Instead of succumbing to the problems and avoiding the discomfort, he chose to hunt it. He didn't accept the "reality" that his restaurant had to close its doors for good. He committed to keeping his staff and the business going—not because he had millions in the bank but because he had faith that he would figure out what to do with his team. Staying accountable and working with his team, he Flipped challenges head-on.

The waitstaff could no longer serve tables, but they *could* deliver to customers' homes. Embracing the reality of food shortages and unreliable transportation chains (remember, this was a time when it was hard to get toilet paper), he created limited menus featuring only the foods he knew he could get. Instead of pulling back on the high-end experience, he doubled down by creating at-home food experiences with spa-night menus, special wine pairings and suggestions for bringing the Addo experience into the safety of one's own home.

The results?

At a time when over 100,000 restaurants permanently closed across the United States, over 2.3 million restaurant jobs were lost, and hundreds of billions in revenue was wiped from the sector,[4] Addo was doing better than ever. Sales were actually higher than when the doors were open, and Eric even had to double his staff to keep up!

If a restaurant can, despite being in one of the toughest businesses during one of the roughest times in the century, create breakthrough success, imagine what might be possible for you.

It Works to Create the Greatest Concentration of Athletic Talent Ever . . .

Jim Ryun was a world record runner and Olympic favorite for the 1968 Summer Olympics in Mexico City. He had the best coaches, equipment and training, and yet he was beat in the 1,500-meter race by a relatively unknown competitor, Kipchoge "Kip" Keino from Kenya.[5] Keino wasn't a professional athlete, he was a police officer who squeezed in his training at night after shifts. Not only did Keino win, he won by still the largest margin in Olympic history, while suffering from a very painful and potentially fatal gallbladder condition.[6]

Over the next few decades, other Kenyans, mostly from the same Kalenjin tribe, won race after race in the competitive running world. "Kenyan runners dominated the sport, winning nearly 70 percent of professional races while only representing 0.06 percent of the world's population,"[7] according to Josh Linkner in his latest book, *Big Little Breakthroughs*. "The oddity is so pronounced, it would be as perplexing as learning that 98 percent of the greatest American chess players all came from one specific neighborhood in Wichita, Kansas."

Sports Illustrated senior editor David Epstein wanted to get to the bottom of this statistical mystery in his book *The Sports Gene: Inside the Science of Extraordinary Athletic Performance*. "There are 17 American men in history who have run under 2:10 in the marathon," he writes. "There were 32 Kalenjin who did it in October of 2011."[8] He conducted research that spanned genetics, body composition and environment. In the end, he concluded that this "greatest concentration of elite athletic talent ever in any sport, anywhere in the world" came down to their ability to run through adversity, to keep going despite the pain and to withstand very high levels of discomfort.[9]

Epstein found that the Kalenjin intentionally cultivate their capacity to handle high levels of discomfort through communal ceremonies where, starting from a young age, individuals undergo painful endurance trials that teach them to endure greater and greater levels of pain. Participants are taught to remain stoic, otherwise they will be socially ostracized.[10] These ceremonies are deeply valued and viewed as a rite of passage from one point in life into another. In many ways, this rite of passage contains many parallels to the hero's journey.

Now, I'm not suggesting you go out and implement painful trials for you or anyone else, but it's clear that both moving through discomfort and acclimating to high levels of discomfort through these rites of passage ceremonies produces incredible, if not seemingly impossible, results.

Much of Western culture, on the other hand, is focused on avoiding struggle, pursuing happiness and avoiding risk at all costs. These days, I can take meetings without going outside thanks to Zoom, have food delivered any time twenty-four hours a day, have endless entertainment at my fingertips, and pop a pill if I'm not feeling well, can't focus or feel anxious. There is a comfort epidemic sweeping Western nations.

You have a choice, though. You can choose discomfort instead of being addicted to the easy way out. You can hunt discomfort—and the five practices described in this book will help you do it. The journey can, and probably will, be downright painful from time to time. The mental, physical, emotional and even spiritual strain might push you in entirely new and uncomfortable ways. The reward is a stronger, better and faster you. And the longer you walk this path, the better equipped you'll be to handle whatever unknown might be around that next corner.

Creating Discomfort to Hunt

Maybe you've hunted all the discomfort that you could find. You addressed the inaccurate views you've had about yourself, others and the world to the best of your ability. You've navigated the waters of self-doubt and exposure. You've used challenges to your advantage, and you're constantly practicing Surrender. What now?

The ambitious can up the ante. It's no longer about finding points of friction around you. It's about creating them. Yes, you did read that right. It's creating circumstances that will force you to address new discomfort, even in small ways. Remember, this is a mountain with no top. If you're committed to sustained growth, then start generating situations that move you deeper into the unknown. It still might not feel very good, but it will get easier as you become a more advanced discomfort practitioner.

Not only will you get better at managing discomfort, you'll get smarter. "Stability [i.e., comfort] is a shut off switch for your brain." Jessica Stillman writes in her article "Science Has Just Confirmed That If You're Not Outside Your Comfort Zone, You're Not Learning," which chronicles Yale University's latest research.[11] "That means crazy, unstable situations might be uncomfortable, but they're also essential if you want to make the most of your brain."

According to five-time entrepreneur Auren Hoffman, cited in Stillman's article, "to maximize learning you need to make sure you're doing hard things [i.e., discomfort] 70 percent of the time."

So, how do you generate some additional discomfort?

You can shorten your timelines. Raise your goals. Broaden your reach. Acclimating to higher levels of discomfort will give you a competitive advantage, and your future self will thank you as you become better prepared for whatever life throws at you next, because difficult times make us stronger, better and faster.

Many of us intuitively know this already. I was listening to the *SmartLess* podcast in which LeBron James expressed the natural wish of all parents: that their kids have a good life. But he also hoped that they have their own challenges, to give them the hunger to go further.[12]

Our obsession with chasing comfort and happiness is leading us down the wrong road. Consider what is, for many, the ultimate dream: winning the lottery. We still believe this, even though many of us have heard the statistic that 70 percent of people who win a lottery or receive a large windfall of money go bankrupt within a few years. According to the research conducted by Harvard Medical School professor Sanjiv Chopra, this is because circumstances like winning the lottery impact only short-term happiness. In the long run, people revert to their own set point.[13]

But our set point doesn't have to be a lifelong sentence. It can be changed, just not with money, accolades, or followers. It has to be achieved through working for it. The only way to reliably achieve sustainable happiness, money or any other result of value is through true growth within yourself. True growth that comes from hunting and conquering discomfort.

The Infinite

Now we're going to ride the pendulum swing from creating discomfort, all the way over to the other side of life, when everything seems to be crashing down around you. During the pandemic, when it felt like the whole world was falling apart, I thought a lot about what it means to hunt discomfort. I thought about my North Star—what was it that would help me navigate my way through this seemingly apocalyptic storm?

Doing this reminded me of something one of my mentors Richard Condon shared with me. He introduced me to the teachings of theologian Paul Tillich, who, in his book *Dynamics of Faith*, identifies two kinds of concerns, or two kinds of matters of importance for humans: finite and ultimate.[14]

Finite concerns are related to specific goals and achievements we want to reach, and we usually know how and when we expect them to be accomplished. Think financial goals, health goals and relationship goals. Finite matters of importance are necessary, and they're great to go after, but they're not necessarily a guiding light, especially when circumstances come crashing down. For that, you need the second matter of importance that Tillich refers to. Ultimate, or infinite.

Ultimate, or infinite, matters of importance transcend the minutia of our day-to-day lives and are the drivers of our values, beliefs, goals, mindsets and emotions. They're things like love, generosity, joy, excellence (not perfection) and spirit.

"Inspiration from those sources can always be trusted," Condon says. "Always."[15] Its purpose transcends your numbers, your strategy and even your being. And it's your guiding light at your darkest moments, no matter what.

When you bring profound love into a fight with your significant other, what happens?

When you bring generosity into a meeting to raise capital, what happens?

When you bring joy into a conversation about the last three quarters' results being down, what happens?

The trick is, it's often most helpful when you least want to call on it. Being generous when you need money is hard. Exhibiting love during a fight is hard. Finding joy in the face of large losses is hard.

This process of bringing your ultimate concerns to finite problems builds your muscle to turn that discomfort into hope. That pain into peace. That embarrassment into generosity. That despair into stead-fastness. And even that worry into resilience. It's something to con-stantly improve upon, not something you'll ever get perfect. (Hint: Don't wait until you're in the darkest times to start, though late is better than never.) It gives you the ultimate power, the power of alignment, because you've calibrated your compass to your true north.

Discomfort	Standard response (fear-based)	#NoMatterWhat response (inspiration-based)
Facing reality	Denial, anger, grief, defensive	Inquisitive, daring, courageous
Self-doubt	Resignation, sadness, false bravado	Committed, powerful, inspired
Exposure	Worried, secretive, inauthentic	Accountable, open, authentic
Challenges	Annoyed, frustrated, resigned	Curious, innovative, confident
Unknown	Controlled, uninspired, insecure	Loving, grateful, graceful

Figure 12.2 #NoMatterWhat Practices

Takeaways

- The five practices for hunting discomfort work together as a process.

- The process of hunting discomfort is a "mountain with no top" (i.e., never-ending).

- The process of hunting discomfort was inspired by the hero's journey archetype.

- If you have hunted all the discomfort around you, create new discomfort.

- Finding the values that really matter to you will guide you when nothing else can.

CHAPTER 13

Join the #NoMatterWhat Movement

Alone we can do so little;
together we can do so much.

—Helen Keller

HUNTING DISCOMFORT IS NOT A FAST GAME, it's a long game. We absolutely must go together if we are going to get there. We need others. Maybe this idea sounds familiar. It should. You read in chapter 7 about forming your Street Gang—the people who have your back and support your growth, especially during the darkest times.

There are entrepreneur groups, faith-based groups, community groups. There are groups for your success and groups for failure, groups for sickness, groups for health, for your age and your ethnicity. Not to mention groups for improving your sport or developing your art. Show me someone who has achieved any meaningful transformation all on their own and I'll show you a liar.

The #NoMatterWhat approach started from an impulse during a time when I needed to dig myself out of a hole. No, more than that, I needed to know *why* I'd fallen so catastrophically, what I did to cause it and how to ensure I learned from it so I wasn't dealing with the same problem in the future. I needed help. I didn't have the people, the connections, the resources or support that were necessary to achieve these aims, and I knew it. That was when I first realized that I needed my own Street Gang. So I started asking for support and offering what I was learning in return. Many of these learnings are now captured in this book.

The founding member of my Street Gang was my sister, Haviland. Seemed fitting, since she was the one who listened to the 1,001 revisions of my Singapore keynote speech during my preparations all those years ago. Seeing as she was my first official Gang Member, I started by sharing with her the discomfort I was going through and how necessary that discomfort was. I still do.

Without my asking or even suggesting it, she started hunting discomfort in her own life. In the face of self-doubt about her body image, she became a professional bodybuilder. She totally transformed her physical activity, her eating and, of course, her body. Today, she runs all the marketing and operations for my speaking and workshop business, and I still wouldn't be doing this without her.

After some time, others saw our achievements and they asked, "What happened?!" And we shared. Slowly, some of our friends started hunting discomfort and creating massive shifts in their lives. Then their friends. And *their* friends. And on it went.

These people started implementing the Hunting Discomfort principles in their own lives and businesses. I was blown away by their courage to move through discomfort. And they too started seeing results—getting new (and higher paying) jobs, starting companies (after sitting on ideas for years), and reporting more joy, happiness and fulfillment in their lives. Still others noticed. They wanted in on the secret. So we shared what we were learning with them. And our circle grew and grew. Before we knew it, we had a community. A community committed to goals, accountability, challenges and results, affectionately (and appropriately) named the #NoMatterWhat Community.

This is not a place for shaming or merely showing off. People in this group are simply committed to moving through discomfort to get to the other side, no matter what that means for them. I couldn't do this without them. You shouldn't have to either.

Enough Is Enough

Although it is true that the world is chock-full of groups, the vast majority of them don't really get to the heart of creating change. Their purpose is for fun or socializing. Those can be fantastic; they just won't make much of a difference.

You can tell if you're part of a change-making group rather than a social one with a simple litmus test in the form of a question. Ask someone how they're doing and listen to their response. If you hear any version of "fine," "good" or "alright," chances are you're in a social group. Because if you're like 100 percent of the other humans on the planet, everything is not always fine.

I moved to Denver late in 2020. There's a pond right by my new house where I enjoy spending time and watching the ducks. They are such peaceful little birds—gliding around on the water, graceful and calm, like they don't have a care in the world. But take a peek at what's happening beneath the water and that illusion is shattered. They are working those legs hard! It's not so idyllic seen from that angle.

In many groups, people show up just like the duck. Maybe you do, too. You participate, act great, maybe even enjoy yourself on the surface of it, but underneath you're paddling like crazy. Mentally. Physically. Emotionally. In your family. With your job. Maybe with your health. If anything, those kinds of surface interactions can even leave you paddling harder in order to keep up the appearance that all is well and hide that pain down below where no one will see it.

Sure, you can get by. You've made it this far, and you'll make it further, just like the duck. But when is enough enough? When have you reached the point where you're done hiding your challenges? When have you reached the point where pretending to be okay is no longer okay? And when are you going to stop trying to get by and instead step into your potential?

How about now?

How about this moment right here?

Write down somewhere: Enough is enough! I WILL _____ #NoMatterWhat.

Fill in the blank above by writing down what you're committed to transforming in your business or in your life. And then write down when you'll do it by. Here's where the difference will be made: share it with your Street Gang or share it with the #NoMatterWhat Community. You can find and join the #NoMatterWhat Community by going to SterlingHawkins.com.

We're never going to arrive at a perfect time, a perfect place or a perfect situation. Declaring that *now* is the time for change doesn't mean that the work is over. It means that right now is a turning point and the work is finally beginning. Why? Because you're willing to make it a turning point. That's all it takes.

You can skip over this section, tell yourself you'll do it tomorrow, or that you have to think about what you really want. You can do that, but know that it's a cop-out. Getting it perfectly right doesn't matter. Taking a stand does. Because when you take a stand for yourself in any area of your life, you spark change that spreads into all the other parts of your life, until you are ablaze with possibility.

All of this from a few simple words?

Yes. Words are powerful and can forever change you. That's why they are one of the ways to Get a Tattoo. Words can awaken inspiration. "Inspiration awakens us to new possibilities by allowing us to transcend our ordinary experiences and limitations," says Scott Barry Kaufman, scientific director of the Imagination Institute in the Positive Psychology Center, at the University of Pennsylvania. "Inspiration propels a person from apathy to possibility, and transforms the way we perceive our own capabilities."[1]

When you begin to participate in the powerful process unleashed by words and inspiration, get ready. You're finally going to do what you were put on this planet to do. And you are going to take steps toward that starting now. And as you do, your words, inspiration and action will in turn inspire others. That's how community works.

CHAPTER 14

Success Stories from the #NoMatterWhat Community

It always seems impossible until it is done.

—Nelson Mandela

I'M CONSTANTLY INSPIRED BY THE #NoMatterWhat Community members. I can't say enough about how fundamental a role they play in keeping me going, especially when things get hard in my life. As much as I've gained from doing this work myself, I've received more inspiration, ideas and strength from witnessing what others are achieving.

The following are stories of real people from the #NoMatterWhat Community who have applied the five practices for transformative results. After each story, I describe standard approaches (as opposed to the Hunting Discomfort approach) they might have taken but which would have left them stuck. These hypothetical standard steps reflect what many of us do most of the time.

It doesn't mean we never deal with our discomfort, but we so often fall short of actively leaning into it in order to move fully through it.

Some of the personal names in these stories have been changed. Everything else is 100 percent true.

Hunting the Discomfort of Reality

After Michelle experienced extreme health issues for several years, her marriage started falling apart just as they had their first child. Her husband started drinking excessively and became angry and abusive. She could finally sleep again after the health scare, but now she was afraid to go to bed, unsure of what her husband might do to her during the night. It was bad enough for her, but their daughter was also exposed to it.

Michelle felt at a loss for what to do. Her husband had been her best friend. They'd been together since high school. She couldn't understand how this could be happening, especially after going through such a serious health concern together. Attempting to just make everything okay, Michelle tried to spend a happy Easter together. Easter morning, instead of hiding eggs and participating in the celebration, her husband hit the gin and yelled about Michelle's inadequacies to her face in front of their daughter.

Michelle was ready. She moved out in secret with her daughter and filed the divorce paperwork.

Hypothetical Response—Deal with the Problem, but Not with the Discomfort

Michelle could have moved in with a friend and returned to work like nothing had happened. She may have started therapy and immediately jumped back into dating as a distraction. She might have been that woman who was determined that everything would be fine—her work, her daughter, her life—and then bury herself in work to just keep "moving ahead." She could have been content with survival—no need to dwell on the past, just keep your head down and keep moving forward.

#NoMatterWhat Response

Michelle's friends came to the rescue by offering her their places to stay. The friends knew Michelle needed the support because she had finally confided in them about what was going on. She initially told people at work she was fine but quickly realized that her feelings didn't match her words. She found the courage to start telling the truth about how she was doing, even though she was in a tender place, because she knew it was the first step out of denial and into the acceptance of her new reality. Letting people into how she was really doing allowed those around her to support her so she could move forward and not stay stuck in the situation. (It was also the beginning of her Street Gang.)

She had started drinking alcohol after the separation to numb her pain, but stopped when she realized that drinking was just a form of escape. Instead of denying her emotions, she explored them fully in somatic therapy. She didn't push the sadness away or the fear about what was next, even when the pain was overwhelming. She allowed all her emotions to move through her.

On the other side of her emotional agony was a new mental clarity. Getting there had taken acceptance, surrender and constantly opening herself up to the possibility of a new reality for herself. Working through what was actually possible (not what she felt was possible from the limited view she had had), she started to take authentic steps into her new reality.

Today, Michelle is the head of global marketing for a Fortune 100 company, is raising her lovely daughter and has found a peace that she has "never known before." Sometimes she is still in disbelief that life can be so good, but she also knows that this is her new life—she is operating from a new baseline. She's still not drinking, has joined several social groups and has just adopted a new puppy. She's lighter, optimistic and more joyful—with a new life, one even better than she could have imagined.

Having your identity decimated can feel like you're dying. Literally. If you remember from chapter 3, it's totally disorienting because who you are today might be tied to your work, your relationships or your social status. None of that is who you really are and, worse, it may be trapping you in a reality that you don't want for yourself. It may feel excruciating to let go, but when you do, you will find that you are not falling, you are flying.

Hunting the Discomfort of Self-Doubt

Soph escaped persecution in Cambodia by coming to the United States with his parents at a young age. When they landed, they didn't have anything and struggled to get by. Soph grew up in the projects, barely spoke English and was challenged in school. So challenged, he dropped out. He lived paycheck to paycheck, eventually married, had two kids and was barely getting by. But that was just how life was, right? Soph had only ever known challenge; he didn't believe he deserved more and was crippled by self-doubt. As the children grew, so did his expenses, so he just took on more jobs, until he was working almost every waking hour of his life. He lived for years this way, with no time off, no friends or social life—he didn't even have time to care for his health. It was hard for him to not become resigned or sad, due to not only his circumstances but also his inability to change his life. He felt powerless.

Hypothetical Response—Deal with the Problem, but not with the Discomfort

Knowing he needed a change, Soph could have called one of his bosses to ask for more work hours so he could let go of one (or two) of his other jobs. Sure, what he really wanted was to start his own business, but he might have focused on the many reasons he couldn't—no schooling, his accent, no time. He could have pushed himself to get his GED (high-school equivalency certification) through tremendous effort and that would have allowed him to ask for a small raise in due time. He could then make a few extra dollars and save a bit for the future. He could easily have seen this life with a bit more cash and a bit less pressure as a successful one.

#NoMatterWhat Response

It was time for a change. Soph's self-doubt triggered deep fear when it came to the prospect of starting a business, going back to school or getting speech therapy, but in identifying those things he was afraid to commit to, he saw the path forward.

The first step on the path was Getting a Tattoo with language. Soph said to himself, "I will be a successful entrepreneur." Then he told this to his wife and friends. Then he figured out the many steps he would have to take to get there. He worked extra hours at his job, using the funds for speech therapy. Once that was completed, he started taking business classes.

A few short years later, he was filing the paperwork for his very first business: a Cambodian beef jerky company, which he started with his wife. He kept his full-time job while he worked nights to produce the jerky and build the business, the entire time never letting go of his dream and never ceasing to repeat his Tattoo to his friends and family. At first they were his only customers, but then local business picked up and online reviews spread the news.

Soph's business is booming. He just bought an Audi R8 and a new home for his family, and can't stop smiling. It's an entirely different life for him now and one that wouldn't have been possible without his hunting the discomfort of self-doubt.

Language is fundamental to how we interpret the world around us. And if it's that powerful, we can use it to draw a line in the sand and mark a turning point. Soph is a great example, declaring to his wife and friends: "I will be a successful entrepreneur." A Tattoo he got before even knowing the business he would start.

The #NoMatterWhat Community is full of people Getting Tattoos and committing to change. One of the first members, Emanuel Mercapidez, actually went to a tattoo shop and got a tattoo of the name of the business he wanted to start, Leftspire, on his bicep—now that's a commitment! Leftspire is now a six-figure marketing business. That's exactly the kind of Tattoo you want to get: one that forces you to commit, with no going back.

Hunting the Discomfort of Exposure

Mark had all the answers. He was sure that the political party he supported was right. He knew the best way for businesses to get back to the office during the pandemic. He even knew what kinds of outfits look best on people, even though he's not in the fashion world. Despite having all the answers, people just weren't listening to him. For some reason, he was living a pretty mediocre life as a vice president at a regional company, with no close friends and no romantic prospects. He couldn't understand why he wasn't being promoted and why the girl of his dreams wasn't walking through the front door. Even worse, deep down he wondered if it was because people knew he was a fraud. But Mark lived the perfect life on the outside, what more could he do?

Hypothetical Response—Deal with the Problem, but not with the Discomfort

Mark could have doubled down on putting himself out there, posting more on social media, resulting in an uptick in his followers. He could have shared some of his ideas with his boss (even though that would be a little uncomfortable), and the company may have even started implementing some of them. Mark might have even taken the leap of starting a fashion blog. Even if he did all that, it didn't mean Mark had started addressing his fear of having to be perfect in order to be accepted. So, no matter how much positive feedback he might have received from others, he wouldn't be able to shake the fact that if anyone saw past his facade, it would all fall apart. His life could have been about finally putting himself out there but still feeling as lonely as ever.

#NoMatterWhat Response

Rather than focusing on getting "out there," Mark turned inward. He recognized that the first step in addressing his fear of exposure involved other people. He called several friends and family members, asking them to fill different roles in his Street Gang.

The first bit of advice from his new mentor was to seek out and resolve some relationships that have been damaged due to his unwillingness in the past to listen. So Mark called a former friend who he had blocked on social media when their political views clashed. Mark asked this person to share more about his perspective and, for once, Mark listened rather than talked. As a result, he was able to view the world more from that person's perspective. It was uncomfortable and destabilizing. All of Mark's absolutism was suddenly replaced with a more complicated and nuanced view of the world. Good thing he had The Heart (his mom) in his Street Gang to help him through it.

Mark kept going. He asked his boss for a meeting, not to share all his good ideas but to ask why things were done a certain way. He was surprised at how interesting the conversation was, and it naturally led to his discovering that some of his business approaches were outdated.

Mark finally turned his newfound curiosity, and openness to see things in a different light, onto himself. He hired an accountability coach and even got into a relationship. He began to form true friendships, based on his newfound openness and vulnerability. His boss called to offer him a raise because his questions (not his answers) had helped the company grow by over 20 percent in just a few months.

Standing on the sidelines of life, it's easy to have all the answers. Watching a soccer game, you might be able to criticize every player on your team, but could you actually do what you're telling them? Probably not. And that's what makes a difference: actually doing something.

Real answers about what to do come from conversations, best had with your Street Gang. It's easy to point fingers and blame someone else. It's easy to say "I told them" or "I tried" or "They just won't listen to me." But that won't help much if you're looking for answers. What *will* help is Building a Street Gang with the mentorship, inspiration, love and accountability you need, and then taking action on the real answers that emerge.

Hunting the Discomfort of Challenges

Jennifer was a super-successful business executive at a Fortune 100 company, making a six-figure salary. She lived in a beautiful home with her husband and kids, whom she adored. But as perfect as her life sounds, she had a significant challenge that no one else knew about—not even her loving family. She was in debt to the tune of almost 1 million dollars from a bad business decision made years ago. Jennifer made her debt payments every month, but it seemed likely she'd be doing that for the rest of her life. Not only that, the secrecy and shame was taking a massive toll on her. She felt stressed, guilty, ashamed and stuck.

Hypothetical Response—Deal with the Problem, but not with the Discomfort

Jennifer is a smart woman. She could have decided to bring her professional expertise to this situation and reduce her expenses by implementing a strict budget every month, convincing her husband to mortgage the house for a better rate than she was paying on her debt—without telling him why. She could have picked up some consulting work on the side so that when she did the math again, instead of it taking forty years to pay off her debt, she would be clear a number of years sooner.

#NoMatterWhat Response

Jennifer decided to Flip It. She started by doing a deep dive into her actual challenge. As she dissected the problem, she realized that she was dealing with the symptom of being embarrassed about her financial mistakes, not the core challenge of actually paying off the debt. No wonder she wasn't making good progress paying it off!

Once Jennifer knew what the actual problem was, she could do something about it. She started by telling her husband. She was sweating, even nauseous talking about it at a certain point, but she made it through. Her husband was furious, and it took weeks to work through the repercussions of her lying to him through omission for so many years. But Jennifer was all-in at this point; there was no going back. She started talking with her Street Gang (see how handy they are everywhere?), and her mentor asked Jennifer to work with her son, who was experiencing some financial trouble. Jennifer did, and in that very moment realized there may be others like her in the same situation whom she could help. She worked with another. And another. And was being paid for her service.

Jennifer trained to become a wealth manager and supplemented her income with this work. She will pay off her debt in less than half the time she had expected to. And the peace and pride that she feels in place of shame and stress is a benefit that one can't put a price tag on.

The way out is always through—or at least the fastest, most efficient and most transformative way out. Of course, that way is never easy. It's incredibly hard to share your darkest challenges and the things you're most ashamed of. I know from my own personal experience.

Hunting the Discomfort of Uncertainty

Helene Hagadorn-Edgerton was dying. One minute she was living her life to the fullest—in her seventies, financially set, feeling great, loving life and most especially her family and grandkids. The next moment, she was sitting in a doctor's office receiving a cancer diagnosis and the news that it had already metastasized throughout her body. She had three months left. Just like that, she was facing the ultimate unknown.

Hypothetical Response—Deal with the Problem, but not with the Discomfort

Helene could have waited to let her loved ones know her health diagnosis because she didn't want to worry them. When she couldn't keep it a secret any longer, she might have told them that she wanted to go out with a celebration, having as much fun as possible. She could have been the person who didn't want to bring people down by talking about uncomfortable things and making everyone feeling uncomfortable. Everyone might have admired her for her determinedly positive attitude, and she may have accepted an antidepression prescription from the doctor and found that helpful. She could have got her affairs sorted behind the scenes, and battled the fear and loneliness quietly on her own. Helene could have kept busy and made keeping others happy her priority right until the end.

#NoMatterWhat Response

This story is actually about my grandmother. I remember that she told us right away about her diagnosis. The next weeks were spent poring through old photographs of her family and reminiscing. She got her affairs in order, but not privately: some hard conversations had to be held with family, but they were necessary so that nobody was surprised or caught off guard by her wishes for her funeral arrangements and disbursement of her possessions. She even called everyone she knew and said goodbye—acknowledging she wouldn't be around much longer.

Most importantly to her, she surrendered to a greater purpose in her passing. In doing so, she modeled for my siblings and me how to love life and let go at the same time, how to die with honor and grace. She was honest about how it wasn't always easy—letting go brought up feelings of grief and vulnerability but also of love and peace. When her time finally came, she left her family forever transformed for the better. It wasn't just the amazing life that she lived that made such an impact, it was how she left it, too.

I'm forever grateful to my grandmother for showing me the way.

Throughout my entire life, my grandmother was always a source of love that I could draw on. We're all capable of doing extraordinary things—even through the last moments we have on this planet. See yourself in these stories. In the discomfort. And in their triumphs. Will you be among those brave enough to step out of your head and into your heart?

Write Your Own Success Story

According to the Buddha, the biggest mistake in life is thinking that you have more time. None of us knows when our time will come—or what unknown might pop up next. But we can choose to befriend this discomfort in order to prepare ourselves for any of it. Remember the adage *memento mori*—what we commit to with our lives here and now will determine what we look back on to celebrate or regret. Live whatever you have big, bold and unflinchingly, no matter what you're facing.

You've taken time out of your life to read this book, time that you will never get back. I appreciate your generosity and hope that you'll be able to take these ideas and apply them in ways that make a difference—I know that I, and many others, have. At the end, this is only a view of reality. Take what works and leave the rest, no harm, no foul. You're responsible for what comes next, and you have to make the best choices for yourself. If you need help, I'm only a click away.

I hope you'll join the hundreds of thousands of us who have embraced these ideas and experienced the profound fulfillment that comes when outcomes align with goals. And as you take steps toward your big dreams and ambitions, you will discover what we all have: that the unpredictability of the world is no match for your creativity, determination and authentic inspiration.

As taught by many people, many religions and many leaders throughout time, but maybe best summed up by Mahatma Gandhi: "If you want to change the world, start with yourself." The path within, to face your own discomforts and move through them, is the path to real change. As you hunt discomfort, the hinted at but maybe unknown potential inside you will become realized. All the unknown elements in your life will transform from intimidating to innovation, from breakdown to breakthrough, and from discomfort to discovery.

When you're brave enough to hunt discomfort, it will show. It will show in your results, and it will show in who you become. People will see it and ask "What happened?!" And you can share. Not too many people enjoy hunting discomfort, but nearly everyone (everyone who I have met) enjoys the results. And by your sharing the results—especially who you are on the other side—the process will become contagious. Like a pebble thrown into a pond, your bravery will have a ripple effect that extends far and wide—into your family, your business, your community, your country and, yes, even the world. Where this impact ends you may never know, but know it's there. By changing yourself, you have changed the world.

There's nothing you can do about what has happened early in your life, a few years ago or even yesterday. But from right now onward, only you have the ultimate say. I invite you to be courageous enough to hunt discomfort and step into your potential—#NoMatterWhat stands in your way.

Ready?

Aim . . .

Hunt.

Acknowledgments

I WILL NOT BE ABLE TO FULLY CAPTURE on this page how grateful I am to the hundreds, if not thousands, of people who have contributed to me over the years and to this book specifically. There are so many people to acknowledge, I'd definitely be getting the hook if this were an awards show. This book is because of them, and in a way even by them. I just put it together. In no particular order:

To Mrs. Muench, my kindergarten teacher, who showed me how to practice, practice, practice every day.

To Steve Stechyshyn (Stech), my high-school accounting teacher cum powerlifting coach, for years of weightlifting and life advice to forge ahead, no matter what.

To Ken Bruer, Richard Condon, John Patterson, Kirkland Tibbels, Matthew Watherston, Abbie Weiss and countless others who have facilitated my training and development over the years and continue to shape me.

To friends who never stop inspiring me, like Sam Abraham, Mina Afshar, Elke Cooke, Steve Dennis, Conal Doyle, Terry Hawkins (no relation, believe it or not), Trey Holder, Christopher Kai, Sabrina Kay, Johnny King, Alexis Kolpak, Matt Ratner, Eric Rodriguez, Matthew Rosenberg, Chris Stauffer, Sandra Vergara and Waldo Waldman.

To Josh Linkner and 3 Ring Circus—a constant source of learning, development and creativity.

To the Coachmasters Toastmasters Club: Sarah Anassori, Isabelle Birdi, Hartmut Eggert, Yvette Frontera, Charlotte Gray, Jimmy Green, Archie Hill, Gavin Masumiya, Ascanio Pignatelli, Valentina Savelyeva and many, many others, for your profound contribution to my earliest days of speaking.

To Antwon Lincoln, for accepting me to deliver a TEDx Talk—and hasn't stopped pushing me since.

To Richard Schelp, Angela Schelp, Peyton Schelp, Stephen Kirkpatrick and the whole Executive Speakers Bureau. I couldn't ask for a better partner in speaking.

To Maggie Langrick, Joanna Henry and the whole Wonderwell team. I literally couldn't have done this without you.

To the #NoMatterWhat Community and all you're up to constantly—you are forever inspiring to me, and I do what I do because of you: Sophen Aik, Dan Ambrose, Jason Borowicz, Sam Campione, Monica Cristerna, Cari Curtis, Nancy Jackson, Olga Kipnis, Sarah Link, Emanuel Mercapidez, Michiel Reijmer and many others.

To my brother Berkeley, my sister-in-law Sasha, my brother Schuyler and their families. To my young nieces, I can't tell you how much I love you girls.

To Dad, for teaching me more than I think you'll ever even realize and always being there to support me.

To Mom, for instilling in me the drive to hunt discomfort as a young child, which shaped me to be who I am today. Grandma would be proud.

To my sister Haviland, my founding Street Gang member who was there with me during my trough of despair and helped me build my life and business back better—no matter what got in our way.

Notes

Chapter 1: Hunting Discomfort

1   D.G. Maté, *In the Realm of Hungry Ghosts* (Vermilion, 2018).

2   George Markowsky, s.v. "Physiology," *Britannica*, July 20, 1998, updated June 16, 2017, britannica.com/science/information-theory/Physiology. (The human body sends 11 million bits per second to the brain for processing, yet the conscious mind seems to be able to process only 50 bits per second.)

3   Naomi Eisenberger, Matthew Lieberman and Kipling Williams, "Does Rejection Hurt? An fMRI Study of Social Exclusion," *Science* 302 (2003): 290–92, doi: 10.1126/science.1089134.

4   C.N. DeWall et al., "Acetaminophen Reduces Social Pain: Behavioral and Neural Evidence," *Psychological Science* 21, no. 7 (2010): 931–37, doi: 10.1177/0956797610374741.

5   National Safety Council, "Odds of Dying," injuryfacts.nsc.org/all-injuries/preventable-death-overview/odds-of-dying.

Chapter 2: Discomfort #1: Facing Reality

1   Jennifer Van Grove, "The Dress Color Controversy Sparks 10,000 Tweets per Minute," TheStreet, February 27, 2015, thestreet.com/technology/the-dress-color-controversy-sparks-10000-tweets-per-minute-13061985.

2   R.S. Nickerson, "Confirmation Bias: A Ubiquitous Phenomenon in Many Guises," *Review of General Psychology* 2, no. 2: 175–220, doi: 10.1037/1089-2680.2.2.175.

3   Carol S. Dweck, "What Is Growth Mindset?" Renaissance, renaissance.com/edwords/growth-mindset/.

4   John Locke and P.H. Nidditch, *An Essay Concerning Human Understanding* (Clarendon Press, 1979).

5   Robert Evans Wilson Jr., "Are Negative Core Beliefs Wrecking Your Life?" *Psychology Today*, September 13, 2021, psychologytoday.com/us/blog/the-main-ingredient/202109/are-negative-core-beliefs-wrecking-your-life.

6   *Britannica*, s.v. "Karl August Möbius," July 20, 1998, updated April 22, 2021, britannica.com/biography/Karl-August-Mobius.

7   A.S. Cherniawsky and C.B. Holroyd, "High Temporal Discounters Overvalue Immediate Rewards Rather Than Undervalue Future Rewards: An Event-Related Brain Potential Study, *Cognitive, Affective, & Behavioral Neuroscience* 13 (2013): 36–45, doi: 10.3758/s13415-012-0122-x.

8   #NoMatterWhat Workshop, November 26, 2019. A #NoMatterWhat workshop in which I challenged the assumptions of the leadership of a grocery company. Changing the lens of belief right then and there in the workshop can be uncomfortable but massively freeing.

9   C.P. Richter, "On the Phenomenon of Sudden Death in Animals and Man," *Psychosomatic Medicine* 19, no. 3 (May–June 1957): 191–98, doi: 10.1097/00006842 -195705000-00004.

10   C.G. Jung, *Collected Works of C.G. Jung*, vol. 8: *The Structure and Dynamics of the Psyche*, CW 8 Para 415, ed. G. Adler and R. Hull (Princeton University Press, 1970), doi: 10.2307/j.ctt5hhr1w.

Chapter 3: Hunting the Discomfort of Reality: Expand Your Reality

1   Eckhart Tolle, *The Power of Now* (London, Hodder Paperback, 2001), 142.

2   Brian Resnick, "'Reality' Is Constructed by Your Brain: Here's What That Means, and Why It Matters," Vox, June 2, 2020, vox.com/science-and-health /20978285/optical-illusion-science-humility-reality-polarization.

3   Fernando Flores, *Conversations for Action and Collected Essays*, self-published, 62–63.

4   Guy Winch, "Why Certain People Will Never Admit They Were Wrong," November 2, 2018, psychologytoday.com/us/blog/the-squeaky-wheel /201811/why-certain-people-will-never-admit-they-were-wrong.

5   Mairi Mackay, "10 Ideas That Changed the World," December 11, 2008, cnn.com /2008/WORLD/europe/11/21/tenthings.changedtheworld/index.html.

6   Bart de Langhe, Stefano Puntoni and Richard Larrick, "Linear Thinking in a Nonlinear World," *Harvard Business Review*, May–June 2017, hbr.org/2017/05 /linear-thinking-in-a-nonlinear-world.

7   Ingrid S. Følling, Marit Solbjør and Anne-S Helvik, "Previous Experiences and Emotional Baggage as Barriers to Lifestyle Change—A Qualitative Study of Norwegian Healthy Life Centre Participants," *BMC Family Practice* 16, no. 73 (2015): 1, doi: 10.1186/s12875-015-0292-z.

8   Ron Friedman, "Get Your Brain Unstuck," *Harvard Business Review*, July 9, 2014, hbr.org/2014/07/get-your-brain-unstuck.

9   Carl Jung, "Christ: A Symbol of Self," in C.G. Jung, *Collected Works of C.G. Jung*, vol. 9, pt. 2, *Aion: Researches into the Phenomenology of the Self* (Princeton University Press, 1968), 70–71.

Chapter 4: Discomfort #2: Self-Doubt

1   Gail S. Altman, *Beethoven: A Man of His Word—Undisclosed Evidence for His Immortal Beloved* (Anubian Press, 1996).

2   Steven Sasson. All material comes from a personal interview done by the author for this book, June 3, 2020.

3   "Lions Hunting," Alert, January 8, 2020, lionalert.org/predatory-behaviour/.

4   Barbara Markway, "The Upside of Self-Doubt," *Psychology Today*, May 3, 2018, psychologytoday.com/us/blog/shyness-is-nice/201805/the-upside-self-doubt.

5   Courtney E. Ackerman, "12 Tips for Building Self-Confidence and Self-Belief," July 12, 2021, positivepsychology.com/self-confidence-self-belief/.

Chapter 5: Hunting the Discomfort of Self-Doubt: Get a Tattoo

1   "Cortés Burns His Boats," PBS.org, pbs.org/conquistadors/cortes/cortes_doo.html.

2   Leadership retreat led by Richard Condon and Matthew Watherston, August–September 2021, Temple of the Way of Light, Loreto, Peru.

3   "4 Ways to Stop Negative Thinking," McLean, September 14, 2021, mcleanhospital.org/essential/4-ways-stop-negative-thinking.

4   Jeremy Engle, "Do You Have Any Close Friends?" *New York Times*, November 27, 2019, nytimes.com/2019/11/27/learning/do-you-have-any-close-friends.html.

5   B. Schwartz, *The Paradox of Choice: Why More Is Less* (Ecco, 2004).

6   William Breitbart, "Memento Mori, Amor Fati," *Palliative Support Care* 17, no. 3 (June 2021), ncbi.nlm.nih.gov/pmc/articles/PMC6629257/.

7   Bronnie Ware, "The Top Five Regrets of the Dying—A Life Transformed by the Dearly Departing," BronnieWare.com, bronnieware.com/regrets-of-the-dying/.

8   Online Etymology Dictionary, s.v. "Decide," etymonline.com/word/decide.

9   "Longest Marriage," *Guinness Book of World Records*, guinnessworldrecords.com/world-records/longest-marriage.

10   "Dian Fossey: Biography," Dian Fossey Gorilla Fund, gorillafund.org/who-we-are/dian-fossey/dian-fossey-bio/.

11   Viktor E. Frankl, *Man's Search for Meaning: An Introduction to Logotherapy* (Beacon Press, 1962).

12   Danny Klein, "Red Robin's CEO Celebrates with a Burger Tattoo," FSR, February 2017, fsrmagazine.com/chain-restaurants/red-robins-ceo -celebrates-burger-tattoo.

13   Teresa M. Amabile and Steven J. Kramer, *The Progress Principle: Using Small Wins to Ignite Joy, Engagement, and Creativity at Work* (Harvard Business Review Press, 2011).

14   Alysha Tsuji, "The Rock Explains Details behind the Incredible New 'Evolution of the Bull' Tattoo," *USA Today*, August 11, 2017, ftw.usatoday.com/2017/08 /dwayne-the-rock-johnson-new-tattoo-bull-cover-up-evolution-details-story -explain-instagram-photos.

Chapter 6: Discomfort #3: Exposure

1   C.G. Jung, *Two Essays on Analytical Psychology* (Pantheon, 1953), 190.

2   Susan Krauss Whitbourne, "5 Reasons We Play the Blame Game," *Psychology Today*, September 19, 2015, psychologytoday.com/us/blog/fulfillment-any -age/201509/5-reasons-we-play-the-blame-game.

3   Lisa Firestone, "Is Cynicism Ruining Your Life?" *Psychology Today*, December 3, 2012, psychologytoday.com/us/blog/compassion-matters/201212/is-cynicism -ruining-your-life.

4   Victoria Lemle Beckner, "The Key Skill We Rarely Learn: How to Feel Your Feelings," *Psychology Today*, October 12, 2020, psychologytoday.com/us/blog /harnessing-principles-change/202010/the-key-skill-we-rarely-learn-how -feel-your-feelings.

5   Brené Brown, "The Midlife Unraveling," Brenebrown.com, May 24, 2018, brenebrown.com/articles/2018/05/24/the-midlife-unraveling/.

6   James Bartholomew, "The Awful Rise of 'Virtue Signalling,'" *Spectator*, July 7, 2018, spectator.co.uk/article/the-awful-rise-of-virtue-signalling-.

7   Gabor Maté, "The Best Explanation of Addiction I've Ever Heard," FightMediocrity, November 16, 2020, YouTube video, 9:49, youtube.com /watch?v=ys6TCO_olOc.

8   Amy Morin, "There Is a Clear Line between Oversharing and Being Authentic— Here's How to Avoid Crossing It," Forbes.com, October 22, 2016, forbes.com /sites/amymorin/2016/10/22/there-is-a-clear-line-between-oversharing -and-being-authentic-heres-how-to-avoid-crossing-it/?sh=6572e13156e3.

9   Rita Gunther McGrath, "Failure Is a Gold Mine for India's Tata," *Harvard Business Review*, April 11, 2011, hbr.org/2011/04/failure-is-a-gold-mine-for-ind.

10   Leigh Buchanan, "Welcome to the Church of Fail," *Inc.*, November 2021, inc.com/magazine/201311/leigh-buchanan/nixonmcinnes-innovation -by-celebrating-mistakes.html.

11 Glenn Croston, "The Thing We Fear More Than Death," *Psychology Today*, November 29, 2012, psychologytoday.com/us/blog/the-real-story -risk/201211/the-thing-we-fear-more-death.

12 Insiya Hussain et al., "The Voice Bystander Effect: How Information Redundancy Inhibits Employee Voice," *Academy of Management Journal* 62, no. 3 (2019): 828–49, doi: 10.5465/amj.2017.0245.

13 Brakkton Booker, "Ex-Michigan Gov. Rick Snyder and 8 Others Criminally Charged in Flint Water Crisis," NPR, January 14, 2021, npr.org/2021/01/14 /956924155/ex-michigan-gov-rick-snyder-and-8-others-criminally -charged-in-flint-water-crisis.

14 "A Former VW Chief Will Pay the Automaker $13.7 Million over Its Emissions Scandal," *New York Times*, June 9, 2021, nytimes.com/2021/06/09/business /Volkswagen-emissions-Martin-Winterkorn.html.

15 "Kanye West," Capital Xtra, capitalxtra.com/artists/kanye-west/lists /inspirational-quotes/live-performance/.

16 Andre Benz, "7 Reasons You Might Feel Lonely Even though You're Not Alone," Mindclear Integrative Psychotherapy, January 1, 2020, mindclearpsychotherapy .com/7-reasons-you-might-feel-lonely/.

17 Dave Evensen, "Nibbled Plants Grow Back Stronger," Futurity, January 4, 2012, futurity.org/nibbled-plants-grow-back-stronger/.

18 Gary Younge, "Martin Luther King: The Story Behind His 'I Have a Dream' Speech," *Guardian*, August 9, 2013, theguardian.com/world/2013/aug/09 /martin-luther-king-dream-speech-history.

Chapter 7: Hunting the Discomfort of Exposure: Build a Street Gang

1 Stacey Hanke," Three Steps to Overcoming Resistance," Forbes.com, August 4, 2018, forbes.com/sites/forbescoachescouncil/2018/08/14/three-steps-to -overcoming-resistance/?sh=162d6c515eae.

2 Anthony de Mello, *The Song of the Bird* (Doubleday, 1984).

3 Marina Milyavskaya et al., "Inspired to Get There: The Effects of Trait and Goal Inspiration on Goal Progress," *Personality and Individual Differences* 52, no. 1 (2012): 56–60, doi: 10.1016/j.paid.2011.08.031.

4 Ryan Holmes, "Why This CEO Appointed an Employee to Change Dumb Company Rules," Fast Company, March 14, 2017, fastcompany.com/3068931/why-this -ceo-appointed-an-employee-to-change-dumb-company-rules.

5   "Is the Letter on Display That Truman Wrote in Defense of His Daughter's Singing?" National Archives, Harry S. Truman Library & Museum, trumanlibrary.gov/education/trivia/letter-truman-defends-daughter-singing.

6   Sabrina Kay. All material comes from a personal interview conducted by the author for this book, August 6, 2021.

Chapter 8: Discomfort #4: Challenges

1   *MacGyver*, season 1, episode 7, "Last Stand," aired 1986, on CBS (Prime Video), amazon.com/MacGyver-Season-1/dp/B000HL2J0G.

2   "Delivery at the Speed of Life," Research Briefs, CB Insights, July 2, 2021, cbinsights.com/research/zipline-series-d-funding/.

3   "Zipline," Crunchbase, crunchbase.com/organization/zipline-international.

4   "Understanding the Conversation Gap: Why Employees Aren't Talking, and What We Can Do about It," Bravely, learn.workbravely.com/hubfs/Understanding -the-Conversation-Gap.pdf.

5   Adam Grant, "The Easiest Person to Fool," in *Hidden Brain* podcast, 53:51, December 24, 2021, hiddenbrain.org/podcast/the-easiest-person-to-fool/.

6   All material comes from a personal interview conducted for a blog, March 22, 2021, sterlinghawkins.com/blog-1/to-build-you-first-have-to-break.

7   Patrick Vlaskovits, "Henry Ford, Innovation, and That 'Faster Horse' Quote," *Harvard Business Review*, August 29, 2011, hbr.org/2011/08/henry-ford-never -said-the-fast.

8   Vlaskovits, "Henry Ford."

9   Sterling Hawkins, "The Way Through: Making a Difference with What You Believe In," June 5, 2020, YouTube video, 10:05:26, youtube.com/watch ?v=ZRBp2WRBsxo.

10 Plato, *Plato's The Republic* (Books, Inc., 1943). Plato famously wrote: "Our need will be the real creator," which was molded over time into the English proverb "Necessity is the mother of invention."

Chapter 9: Hunting the Discomfort of Challenges: Flip It

1   Diala, "Origin of Nutella," Gaincontact.com, February 5, 2020, gaincontact.com /origin-of-nutella/.

2   D. Cleden, *Managing Project Uncertainty* (Gower, 2009).

3   Magdalaena Osumi, "Hotels in Japan Roll Out Unusual Bids to Woo Tourists in COVID-19 Crisis," *Japan Times*, March 19, 2020, japantimes.co.jp/news/2020 /03/19/business/hotels-japan-unconventional-offers-coronavirus/.

4   This quote is usually attributed to Charles Kettering, who was head of research at General Motors from 1920 to 1947. See brainyquote.com/quotes/charles _kettering_181210.

5   "How Kaiser Permanente Providers Are Paid," Kaiser Permanente, healthy .kaiserpermanente.org/content/dam/kporg/final/documents/health-plan -documents/coverage-information/how-kaiser-permanente-providers-are -paid-ca-en.pdf. "Medical group physicians are rewarded for doing what's right for you, rather than being paid based on the number of services they provide or on their use of referral services. The Medical Group pays physicians a market-based salary, supplemented by small incentives. These incentives are based on several things, including: quick and easy access to appointments, patient satisfaction, and high quality care. These small incentives do not require Health Plan to provide stop-loss protection to its physicians. Medical Group physicians are rewarded for delivering care that helps keep you healthy and productive—the right care at the right time."

6   Marc Brown, "Medicare Plans Rated among the Nation's Best," Kaiser Permanente, October 8, 2020, about.kaiserpermanente.org/our-story/news /accolades-and-awards/medicare-plans-rated-among-the-nations-best.

7   Dubin shared this story at an industry event I attended several years ago. Michael Dubin live presentation, Retail Tomorrow event, Los Angeles, March 20, 2019.

8   John Mannes, "Unilever Buys Dollar Shave Club for Reported $1B Value," TechCrunch, July 19, 2016, techcrunch.com/2016/07/19/unilever-buys-dollar -shave-club-for-reported-1b-value/.

9   "How Britain Invented the Tank in the First World War," Imperial War Museums, iwm.org.uk/history/how-britain-invented-the-tank-in-the -first-world-war.

10   Ted Ryce. All material comes from a personal interview conducted by the author for this book, June 5, 2020.

11   "3 Ring Circus—Keynote Formation: Example Introduction," Vimeo video, 14:28, vimeo.com/362092007/497c9bff71.

12   "Flavor Graveyard," Ben & Jerry's Homemade, benjerry.com/flavors/flavor -graveyard.

13   Richard Branson, *Losing My Virginity: The Autobiography* (Virgin Publishing, 1998), 298.

14   Oguz A. Acar, Murat Tarakci and Daan van Knippenberg, "Why Constraints Are Good for Innovation," *Harvard Business Review*, November 22, 2019, hbr.org/2019/11/why-constraints-are-good-for-innovation.

15   "About Us," Gopuff.com, gopuff.com/go/about-us.

Chapter 10: Discomfort #5: Uncertainty

1   Ricardo Bilton, "Color Goes Dark: Board Votes to Shut Down Company, Source Says (Updated)," VentureBeat, October 17, 2012, venturebeat.com/2012/10/17/more-trouble-for-color-shareholders-and-board-vote-to-wind-down-company/.

2   Michaeleen Doucleff, "Between Pigs and Anchovies: Where Humans Rank on the Food Chain," NPR, December 8, 2013, npr.org/sections/thesalt/2013/12/08/249227181/between-pigs-and-anchovies-where-humans-rank-on-the-food-chain.

3   *Britannica*, s.v. "Hypothesis Testing," July 20, 1998, updated October 20, 2020, britannica.com/science/statistics/Hypothesis-testing.

4   Martyn Shuttleworth and Lyndsay T Wilson, "Type I Error and Type II Error," Explorable, explorable.com/type-i-error.

5   *Britannica*, s.v. "Uncertainty Principle," July 20, 1998, updated June 1, 2021, britannica.com/science/uncertainty-principle.

6   "Boston: A City Steeped in U.S. History," History.com, March 13, 2019, history.com/topics/us-states/boston-massachusetts.

7   Kevin Bartley, "Big Data Statistics: How Much Data Is There in the World?" Rivery, rivery.io/blog/big-data-statistics-how-much-data-is-there-in-the-world/.

8   Martin Heidegger and William Lovitt, *The Question Concerning Technology, and Other Essays* (Harper & Row, 1977).

9   Pat Kinsella, "Leif Erikson's Voyage to Vinland," History Extra, January 13, 2021, historyextra.com/period/viking/who-was-leif-erikson-facts-life-viking-voyage-vinland/.

Chapter 11: Hunting the Discomfort of Uncertainty: Surrender

1   Suraj Iyer, "Simone Biles Is One of the Greatest Gymnasts Ever: But How Does She Train?" The Bridge, May 27, 2021, thebridge.in/fitness-wellness/simone-biles-is-one-of-the-greatest-gymnasts-ever-but-how-does-she-train-21709?infinitescroll=1.

2   Tara Brach, "Soul Recovery," *Psychology Today*, March 28, 2017, psychologytoday.com/us/blog/finding-true-refuge/201703/soul-recovery.

3   Julian D. Ford et al., "The Symptoms of Trauma Scale (SOTS): An Initial Psychometric Study," *Journal of Psychiatric Practice* 21, no. 6 (November 2015): 474–83, ncbi.nlm.nih.gov/pmc/articles/PMC4643404/.

4   Linda B. Buck, "New Studies Examine How Mice Respond to a Predator's Scent," Howard Hughes Medical Institute, March 21, 2016, hhmi.org/news/new-studies-examine-how-mice-respond-predator-s-scent.

5   Mi-Seon Kong et al., "'Fearful-Place' Coding in the Amygdala-Hippocampal Network," eLife Sciences, September 17, 2021, elifesciences.org/articles/72040 .pdf.

6   "Anxiety, Trauma and How Prolonged Exposure Therapy Works for PTSD ft. Dr. Edna Foa," SAMHSA, November 7, 2016, YouTube video, 32:10, youtube.com/watch?v=6L-CCW85n0A.

Chapter 12: The #NoMatterWhat System for Hunting Discomfort

1   "Everest 1953: First Footsteps—Sir Edmund Hillary and Tenzing Norgay," *National Geographic*, March 3, 2013, nationalgeographic.com/adventure /article/sir-edmund-hillary-tenzing-norgay-1953; the quote is from Hazel Plush, "'Life's Like Mountaineering—Never Look Down': The Wisdom of Sir Edmund Hillary, *Telegraph*, July 20, 2016, telegraph.co.uk/travel/destinations /asia/nepal/articles/quotes-sir-edmund-hillary-first-man-climb-everest/.

2   Joseph Campbell, *The Hero with a Thousand Faces*, 3rd ed. (New World Library, 2008).

3   Joe Ray, "While Many Restaurants Struggle, Here's How One Is Thriving," *Wired*, March 24, 2020, wired.com/story/restaurants-struggling -pandemic-eric-rivera-addo/.

4   Andrew Bander, "4 Ways 2020 Left the Restaurant Industry on the Brink of Disaster," Forbes.com, December 21, 2020, forbes.com/sites/andrewbender /2020/12/21/4-ways-2020-left-the-restaurant-industry-on-the-brink-of-disaster /?sh=4c2e0ae857a1; Alicia Kelso, "Restaurant Industry Expected to Lose $240B by the End of 2020," *Restaurant Dive*, June 16, 2020, restaurantdive.com /news/restaurant-industry-expected-to-lose-240b-by-the-end-of-2020/579857/.

5   "Kipchoge Keino," World Sport, CNN.com International, June 23, 2004, edition.cnn.com/2004/SPORT/06/03/olympics.keino/index.html.

6   "Kipchoge Keino," Olympics.com, olympics.com/en/athletes/kipchoge-keino.

7   Josh Linkner, *Big Little Breakthroughs* (Post Hill Press, 2021), 231.

8   Quoted in Gregory Warner, "How One Kenyan Tribe Produces the World's Best Runners," NPR, November 1, 2103, npr.org/sections/parallels/2013/11/01 /241895965/how-one-kenyan-tribe-produces-the-worlds-best-runners.

9   David Epstein, *The Sports Gene: Inside the Science of Extraordinary Athletic Performance: David Epstein* (Portfolio, 2014).

10   Anna Wilgenbusch, "What's in a Game: How You, Me, and a Kenyan Runner See Pain," (University of Dallas) *University News*, September 29, 2019, udallasnews.com/2019/09/29/whats-in-a-game-how-you-me-and-a-kenyan -runner-see-pain/.

11 Jessica Stillman, "Science Has Just Confirmed That If You're Not Outside Your Comfort Zone, You're Not Learning," Inc., August 14, 2018, inc.com /jessica-stillman/want-to-learn-faster-make-your-life-more-unpredictable .html.

12 "LeBron James," episode 52, *SmartLess* podcast, Spotify, 57:25, July 2021, open.spotify.com/episode/6mQhlX4QjyvJexWFsuNdA4.

13 George Loewenstein, "Five Myths about the Lottery," *Washington Post*, December 27, 2019, washingtonpost.com/outlook/five-myths/five-myths-about-the -lottery/2019/12/27/742b9662-2664-11ea-ad73-2fd294520e97_story.html.

14 P. Tillich, *Dynamics of Faith* (Perennial, 2001).

15 Richard Condon, leadership workshop, Temple of the Way of Light, Loreto, Peru, August–September 2021.

Chapter 13: Join the #NoMatterWhat Movement

1 Scott Barry Kaufman, "Why Inspiration Matters," *Harvard Business Review*, November 8, 2011, hbr.org/2011/11/why-inspiration-matters.

Index

About the Author

Sterling Hawkins is out to break the status quo. He believes that we can all unlock incredible potential within ourselves, and he's on a mission to support people, businesses and communities to realize that potential, regardless of the circumstances.

From a multibillion-dollar start-up to collapse and coming back to launch, invest in and grow over fifty companies, Sterling takes that experience to work with C-level teams from some of the largest organizations on the planet and speaks on stages around the world.

Today, Sterling serves as CEO and founder of the Sterling Hawkins Group, a research, training and development company focused on human and organizational growth. He has been seen in publications like *Inc.*, *Fast Company*, *The New York Times* and *Forbes*.

Based in Colorado, Sterling is a proud uncle of three and a passionate adventurer who can often be found skydiving, climbing mountains, shark diving or even trekking in the Sahara. Maybe you'll even join him for the next adventure—and discover the breakthrough results you're looking for. He'll have your back, #NoMatterWhat.

For more information, visit SterlingHawkins.com.

Hunting Discomfort is a journey without an end. This work never stops and neither should you. To that end, I've created bonus content, workbooks and exercises to keep you going with each of the five #NoMatterWhat practices.

And you're not on this hunt alone. You can learn about and join the #NoMatterWhat Community to surround yourself with others who are committed to making a bigger impact and hunting the discomfort necessary to do it.

It's all available at **HuntingDiscomfort.com**.